D0875715

GBS
GKC

GBS
GKC

SHAW and CHESTERTON
The Metaphysical Jesters

William B. Furlong

The Pennsylvania State University Press

University Park and London

Standard Book Number 271–00110–0
Library of Congress Catalogue Card 77–114616
Copyright © 1970 by The Pennsylvania State University
Printed in the United States of America

preface

George Bernard Shaw and Gilbert Keith Chesterton were two of the most skilled "metaphysical jesters" whom God, or the Life Force, ever chose to pair in human debate. The two men shared public platforms for sixteen years (1911–27) and private friendship for at least thirty-five (1901–36). When this century was new, their popularity was such that Chestertonians and Shavians, whole groups of apostles and disciples, sprang up and thrived on both sides of the Atlantic. In Great Britain an editor had only to use the initials "G.B.S." or "G.K.C." to identify either for the general public. The edge of that sort of popularity has long since dulled, especially for Chesterton. Yet it seems odd that so little has been written about a key relationship between two men who were admired by their contemporaries as giants. Perhaps it is odder still that in the present climate of literary studies almost nothing has been written about the significant literary effects each had on the other. How can literary specialists prone to investigate even the minutiae of a period overlook the relationship of two of its most towering figures?

One basic reason for the neglect is quite human and understandable. G.B.S. and G.K.C. simply did not attract mutual friends and advocates. Despite a warm personal friendship that never wavered, Shaw and Chesterton were most often diametrically opposed in principle. Such differences made for excellent debate, but even today the scholar drawn to Shaw is seldom attracted to Chesterton, and the reverse is also true. Whatever the men accomplished in tandem is allowed, for the most part, to moulder quietly in yellowing files.

Although this neglect is inglorious, G.B.S. and G.K.C. would have appreciated that scholars of today recognize the basic differences between them. Such had not been the case in 1911. Then the public had not understood the differences nor had it decided how to react to the pair as a debating team. When the two men mounted a public platform to prick away at the social conscience, the audience would take instinctively the one refuge it may always take from humorous artists—refuse to take them seriously. As Maisie Ward wrote:

> These men were constantly arguing with each other; but the literary public felt all the same that they represented something in common, and the literary public was by no means sure that it liked that something. It could not quite resist Bernard Shaw's plays; it loved Chesterton whenever it could rebuke him affectionately for paradox and levity. What that public succumbed to in these men was their art: it was by no means so certain that it liked their meaning. And so the literary public elected to say that Shaw and Chesterton were having a cheap success by standing on their heads and declaring that black was white. The audience watched a Shaw v. Chesterton debate as a sham fight or a display of fireworks, as indeed it always partly was; for each of them would have died rather than really hurt the other. But Shaw and Chesterton were operating on their minds all the time. They were allowed to sit in the stalls and applaud. But they were themselves being challenged; and that spoilt their comfort.

Whatever its cause, the time has come to break the relative silence on the Shaw-Chesterton relationship. Such couplings of major talent are so rare in literary history that not a moment should be lost before documenting this one. Already, many of the public exchanges, never recorded, have vanished irretrievably. Time is also diminishing swiftly the number of living people who had the privilege to know both men or to hear them debate. It would be a pity if neglect of easily misplaced records should permit other details or even important facts about G.B.S. and G.K.C. to sink into oblivion.

For more is at stake here than an important relationship in the life of Bernard Shaw. Although G.B.S. is a figure of indisputable significance, he himself knew that G.K.C. was not a mere springboard to display his own wit and talent. Rather, Shaw was convinced that G. K. Chesterton was "a man of colossal genius." As Maisie Ward pointed out when she published a second book of memorabilia about G.K.C., "one must not dismiss the possibility that Bernard Shaw may have been right in calling him 'a man of colossal genius.' If this happens to be so, every detail about him is of importance to his own age and still more to posterity, when he will have come finally into his own."[2]

I am grateful to the staff of the Pattee Library at The Pennsylvania State University for making the writing of this first book-length account of the Shaw-Chesterton relationship much easier than it might have been. Professor Stanley Weintraub contributed invaluable advice and information, and the Society of Authors, representing the Shaw estate, permitted the quotation of passages from an unpublished letter. Like many others writing about Chesterton, I am also indebted to Miss Dorothy Collins, his literary executrix, for much prompt and generous assistance.

W.B.F.

contents

GBS
GKC

one

"WHAT ABOUT THE PLAY?"

It is no longer possible to verify such simple but important facts as the time and the place of the first meeting between G.B.S. and G.K.C. Some authors with a sense of history but more zeal than accuracy have misreported the event. Vincent Brome stated firmly that G.K.C. first met G.B.S. in 1901 in Paris in the studio of Auguste Rodin, who was modeling Shaw at the time.[1] Maisie Ward alluded to the same meeting[2] which unquestionably took place, but not in 1901. Rodin himself did not meet Shaw or begin the bust until five years later in April of 1906.[3] On the other hand, it is clear that Shaw had met Chesterton by 1901 at the latest, although we don't know the precise date, hour, and place of the meeting. Some members of the Fabian Society, of which both G.B.S. and G.K.C. were members, think the pair may have become acquainted a year or two before 1901. G.K.C. left the Fabian Society at the time of the Boer War (1899–1902), and it is difficult to conceive the ebullient G.B.S. and the mountainous G.K.C. cavorting about at the same Fabian meetings and *not* knowing each other.

Still, most writers refer confidently to a thirty-five year friendship (1901–36) between G.B.S. and G.K.C., and Shaw himself provided the best evidence that the 1901 date is correct when he wrote: "I cannot remember when I first met Chesterton. I was so much struck by a review of Scott's *Ivan-*

hoe which he wrote for the *Daily News* in the course of his earliest notable job as feuilletonist to that paper that I wrote to him asking who he was and where he came from, as he was evidently a new star in literature. He was either too shy or too lazy to answer. The next thing I remember is his lunching with us on quite intimate terms accompanied by Belloc."[4] Shaw's notation clears the air. Chesterton wrote his piece about Scott in the *Daily News* for August 10, 1901. After that, all the letters exchanged between G.B.S. and G.K.C., all the articles each wrote about the other, signify plainly that the men knew one another.

One settles for 1901 as the year in which G.B.S. and G.K.C. first met, but one can still learn much from the account of that first fully *recorded* meeting in Rodin's studio in 1906. The circumstances were colorful. Lucian Oldershaw, Chesterton's brother-in-law, had taken him to visit François Auguste René Rodin, the leading French sculptor, at his studio in Paris. Chesterton, not quite massive at thirty-two but already impressively large, was arrayed in his bulky theatrical cloak and was brandishing a swordstick. Rodin was busy trying to capture the likeness of Shaw, who, stripped to the waist, refused to remain immobile in his chair but rather, arms flying, was expatiating to the bewildered Rodin on the relative merits of the Salvation Army.

The occasion must have been trying for Rodin. He was a particularly emotional man even for an artist. Most sculptors are moved when they first catch sight of the Parthenon —Rodin fainted. Actually, on this day, in the rush of Shaw's talk, Rodin scarcely had time to be more than momentarily startled by even the contours and grotesque array of a Chesterton. Shaw was engaging his attention on all levels. Perhaps all that saved Rodin from being inundated in talk was that G.B.S. was speaking French and his French was halting. He was quite apologetic when Rodin's secretary explained to him in broken English: "The master says you have not much French but you impose yourself."[5]

At any rate before Shaw could launch into a detailed account of *Major Barbara* (1905) and its Salvation Army background, the monologue stopped while Oldershaw made Rodin and Shaw conscious of G.K.C.'s presence. Then G.B.S. resumed speaking. He discoursed first on paving stones, drainage, and rates, then ranged to Free Trade and the Boer War. Chesterton listened comfortably and said little. He was able to exhibit on this day a trait which Maisie Ward has several times attributed to him, that of being one of the few great conversationalists who would really rather listen than talk. Oldershaw later carped on this point a bit, claiming that Shaw "talked Chesterton down." Actually, in retrospect, it seems perfectly natural that the famous man should have talked more than the beginner.

In recording the meeting, Vincent Brome and Maisie Ward scarcely mention Rodin since their prime purpose was to note the occasion on which Shaw and Chesterton met. Yet Rodin was the pivotal figure in the scene. Shaw's whole verbal performance was for Rodin. On that day G.B.S. was aware that only two men of major and proven creative talent were present, himself and Rodin. G.B.S. was more than willing to admit that, at the time, Rodin was the ranking genius.

Rodin was sixty-six, at the peak of his fame and known as the "Great Master." He did not look the part. Short, bulky, he appeared more like a peasant farmer although he was grave and magisterial in manner. He thought Shaw something of a fraud and poseur. It was only because he saw in Shaw's face an authentic Christ mask that he had let Mrs. Shaw persuade him to do the bust. On the other hand, Shaw's admiration for Rodin was genuine. Archibald Henderson, G.B.S.'s biographer, was present on a later occasion when Shaw gave Rodin a valuable copy of the *Kelmscott*

Chaucer. G.B.S. wrote on the flyleaf of William Morris' *chef d'oeuvre:* "I have seen two masters at work, Morris who made this book / The other Rodin the Great, who fashioned my head in clay; / I give the book to Rodin, scrawling my name in a nook / Of the shrine their works shall hallow when mine are dust by the way."[6]

When Rodin modeled him, G.B.S. was himself a late emerging genius, still on the rise, composing in the mornings of this very year (1906) *The Doctor's Dilemma.* Accomplishments like *Arms and the Man* (1894), *Candida* (1895), *The Devil's Disciple* (1897), and *Caesar and Cleopatra* (1898) were already far behind him. G.B.S. had already peaked once in 1903 with *Man and Superman,* and again in 1905 with *Major Barbara.* The future still held provocative works like *Pygmalion* (1913), *Back to Methuselah* (1920), and the monumental *Saint Joan* (1923). G.B.S. was also in 1906 a superb subject for sculpture.[7] Fifty years of age, six feet four inches tall (two inches taller than Chesterton), lithely erect, eyes alight and roving, he was over-all a handsome, vital man.

If Chesterton at thirty-two represented a third stage, the fledgling genius, the fact was only semi-evident on this afternoon in Rodin's studio. G.K.C. was far from completely unknown. He had struck some excellent journalistic sparks, especially in the *Daily News.* In 1900 he had first attained the dignity of hard-cover literary status with *Graybeards at Play,* a clever enough combination of nonsense rhymes and illustrations, in the manner of Edward Lear. Still, *Graybeards* hardly intimated approaching fame. And an excellent novel, *The Napoleon of Notting Hill* (1904), demonstrated literary ability but had not yet attracted much attention. Fame of many sorts awaited G.K.C., however. Five years after the meeting in Rodin's studio, Shaw and Chesterton would mount a rostrum for their first debate. Ten years after that critics like Hesketh Pearson would hail G.B.S. and G.K.C. as the "Debaters of the Century."

This meeting of G.K.C. and G.B.S. indirectly reveals much about the essential natures of the two men. Journalist Chesterton never so much as mentioned that he had met Bernard Shaw on such a historic artistic occasion. Most young journalists would have rushed into print with an account of such a colorful meeting just as Rainer Maria Rilke had dashed off a letter to his wife and one to a friend on April 19, 1906, breathlessly describing each detail about Rodin at work on Shaw. Again, one can scarcely imagine, for example, the ambivalent T. E. Lawrence (who was not at all ambivalent when it came to matters that affected his fame[8]) taking a cavalier attitude toward his own meetings with G.B.S. Lawrence was perfectly capable of adopting such a stance as part of his process of cultivating Shaw, but with Chesterton the seemingly indifferent attitude was transparently sincere.

Chesterton was completely oblivious to the externals of human encounter. He admired St. Thomas Aquinas and late in his life wrote the best book about the mind of the Angelic Doctor which had yet appeared in the twentieth century. Yet, if by some temporal saltus he had been permitted to meet St. Thomas in person, it is extremely doubtful that he would have remembered so much as the color of his cassock. G.K.C. was the same about Shaw. What still fascinated Chesterton in 1906, and continued to fascinate him, was the detached Shavian intellect. What almost startled Chesterton was his realization that he had encountered in G.B.S. the passionate Irishman personified, yet an Irishman who wasted on Ireland none of the patriotism of the ordinary kind but rather had managed to sublimate all his passion into pure intellectual passion. Of biographical detail about Shaw or anyone else, however, G.K.C. remembered little.

Similarly, G.K.C. had on several occasions been pressed to relate the physical details of his first meeting with Hilaire Belloc, the poet-historian with whom his name has often been coupled. Obligingly, he gave several accounts, all wrong as to the date, place, and circumstances. This was the man who was to wire his wife one bleak Sunday morning: "Am in Manchester. Where should I be?"

Nevertheless, G.K.C. was also on record several times as recognizing that his absent-mindedness and abstractions were not virtues. Such qualities provided titillating and affectionate literary anecdotes about G.K.C., but unfortunately they carried over too often into his art. For example, he was to write later in this year of 1906 a fairly penetrating biography of Dickens (admired by Shaw) in which he did not give a single date. Some found it extraordinary that he could capture as much as he did of the essential Dickens without recourse to factual data, but, in the end, this was something about G.K.C. that scholars found exasperating; too often he needlessly flaunted scholarly procedure.

Turning back to G.K.C. as man rather than artist, he absent-mindedly sold all rights to his book *Orthodoxy* (1908) for one hundred pounds, and literally horrified the business-like Bernard Shaw. Any student of Chesterton will recognize that this behavior was perfectly consistent with his behavior throughout life. Any Shavian will understand that when Shaw took such a man in tow, it had to be on a commanding paternal basis.

Shaw was not only eighteen years older than G.K.C., he had a fundamentally different approach to life. No one enjoyed being "pure mind" more than G.B.S. Unlike Chesterton, however, he could also be immensely practical. Shaw's eye for human detail as a playwright never obscured his eye for business detail. He could be a scourge to theatre managers and publishers. G.B.S. could see and act upon the fine print in a contract. Always Shaw saw what he wanted to see. He had no reason to notice or flatter Chesterton particularly at the meeting at Rodin's; apparently he didn't even remember his presence. In 1906 G.K.C. was still merely a writer of largely unfulfilled promise. G.B.S. was more anxious to impress Rodin, one of the "elect," the man of major creative talent, the superman. The only hierarchy Shaw ever recognized was the hierarchy of the intellect. Later, when Shaw had read more of Chesterton's important writing and realized that G.K.C. had also become one of the "elect," the picture was to change.

Once G.B.S. decided that G.K.C. was "a man of colossal genius," the intimacy between them was never to wane. Conversely, even from the first day the three men dined in company, Belloc's influence over Chesterton did wane. Only three men were to have any real influence over Chesterton's literary career. Of the three, Shaw was the man who disagreed most with G.K.C. in philosophic principle. Yet ironically, of the three, only G.B.S. was to have a completely salutary effect on Chesterton as an artist. For example, Chesterton's younger brother Cecil had been the first man to affect the direction of G.K.C.'s literary effort. Cecil would teach his brother all the political philosophy he would ever learn, and it was enough to insure that G.K.C. could one day engage a certain Bernard Shaw in intelligent political debate. Unfortunately, Cecil more than offset the balance by also enmeshing G.K.C. in several hopeless, dead-end journalistic enterprises that would persist long after his own death in World War I.

Belloc was the second man to affect Chesterton's literary career. Even before Shaw decided to take proprietary interest in G.K.C. as artist, he found it necessary to make publicly evident that Belloc was leading Chesterton down the wrong literary road. It was not that G.B.S. intended to under-

mine Belloc. He liked and admired him. It was rather that
the perceptive Shaw was the first to discern the complete and
dangerous lack of harmony between the men as literary partners. Despite his personal affection for G.K.C., Belloc, with
his severely classical taste, found Chesterton's free style
unpalatable. Belloc admitted he had read few of G.K.C.'s
books. The gaps in the evaluation he wrote of G.K.C.[9]
would seem to confirm his admission. To the public the men
have always remained literary twins despite this evidence to
the contrary. When, in 1905, Shaw referred to them as a
single phenomenon, the "Chesterbelloc," the public quickly
seized on the term as one of approbation, forgetting completely that G.B.S. had employed it only to show how unnatural was the association of the two men. Shaw had declared
bluntly: "Belloc and Chesterton are not the same sort of
Christian, not the same sort of pagan, not the same sort of
Liberal, not the same sort of anything intellectual."[10]

G.B.S. made this statement in the beginning of his now
famous essay "The Chesterbelloc." The essay stands as the
first direct and important literary result of the Shaw-Chesterton controversy. An acute piece of critical writing which was
highly imaginative even for Shaw, the essay started the controversy off on an admirable literary plane. Today Shaw's
overriding image of the striking Chesterbelloc monster tread-
ing its serpentine way still has the power to fascinate. When
G.B.S. wrote the piece, however, he probably had more in
mind than literary approval. G.B.S. disapproved violently the
direction in which "Hilaire Forelegs" was leading the towering "Hindlegs" Chesterton. He was convinced G.K.C. was
following the lead of a lesser man. Shaw was to conclude
his analysis with a worried but ringing challenge: "And now,
what has the Chesterbelloc (or either of its pairs of legs) to
say in its defense? But it is from the hind legs [Chesterton's]
that I particularly want to hear; because South Salford will
very soon cure Hilaire Forelegs of his fancy for the ideals of

the Catholic peasant proprietor. He is up against his problems in Parliament: it is in Battersea Park [where Chesterton
lived] that a great force is in danger of being wasted."

G.B.S. was quite right about the Chesterbelloc. Not
much held it together intellectually, and time soon vindicated
Shaw's qualifications as prophet of its fate. Belloc and Chesterton not only disbanded as an active literary team but also
saw little of each other as friends after G.K.C. moved out of
London in 1909. Contrary to the public's opinion, Belloc
had little tangible influence over Chesterton's conversion to
the Roman Catholic Church in 1922. Rather, he expressed
pleased surprise over the fact that his friend Gilbert had
gone over to Rome.

Shortly after 1905 Bernard Shaw was able to move
to the fore and attempt to influence Chesterton's career
directly. He was certain that he knew where G.K.C.'s prime
talents lay. He was confident that G.K.C. could make his
mark as a practicing playwright. To the public then as to the
public now, the notion of Gilbert Chesterton as a playwright
was foreign. Those Chestertonians or Shavians who are
vaguely aware of Shaw's conviction have quite naturally
regarded it as a side issue in the relationship, as though G.B.S.
considered playwrighting a pleasant avocation for Chesterton. Actually Shaw seriously believed that the writing of
plays should be Chesterton's major occupation in literature.
Although G.K.C.'s output as a dramatist was to be confined
to two plays produced and one unproduced, his potential as
playwright held Shaw's interest between 1905 and 1913.

Maisie Ward says that very early in their friendship
Shaw had begun to urge Chesterton to write a play. By 1908
G.B.S.'s importunings had advanced to such a stage that he
was capable of writing to G.K.C. only half facetiously:

> What about that play? It is no use trying to answer me
> in The New Age: the real answer to my article is the play.
> I have tried fair means: The New Age [the journal in

which "The Chesterbelloc" had first appeared] article was the inauguration of an assault below the belt. I shall deliberately destroy your credit as an essayist, as a journalist, as a critic, as a Liberal, as everything that offers your laziness a refuge, until starvation and shame drive you to serious dramatic parturition. I shall repeat my public challenge to you; vaunt my superiority; insult your corpulence; torture Belloc; if necessary, call on you and steal your wife's affections by intellectual and athletic displays, until you contribute something to the British drama. . . . Nothing can save you now except a rebirth as a dramatist. I have done my turn; and I now call on you to take yours and do a man's work.[11]

Now Shaw began to write insistently to G.K.C. on the subject of composing a play.[12] Unfortunately, the letters did not bear practical fruit. G.K.C. did not write the play, but instead further rebuffed G.B.S. by writing a book, albeit a brilliant one, *George Bernard Shaw,* in 1909. Shaw was temporarily nonplussed although he realized that the book was a literary achievement by any standard. *George Bernard Shaw* was not only a major literary landmark of the friendship, it was also one of the prime examples of the men's fascination with each other, a mutual fascination that was to endure until G.K.C.'s death. Still, the book was not a play, and Shaw chafed at the time Chesterton had devoted to its composition even though he was not insensitive to the flattering implications behind the fact that G.K.C. had written it.

Then, considering his fame and the concomitant demands upon his time, Shaw went to unusual lengths to induce G.K.C. to write a play. In 1909 G.B.S. himself composed an outline scenario (holograph now in the British Museum) which was to serve as groundwork for a complete play by Chesterton. The outline had for a basic theme the return of St. Augustine to the England he had converted. G.B.S. incorporated a scene in heaven in which the Devil, making a periodic visit, convinced St. Augustine that he had better travel to earth to check out whether or not England was still a Christian country. Augustine makes the trip to investigate and encounters in Westminster a humorously literal policeman, a worldly Bishop of Blackfriars, and an effete newspaper tycoon, Lord Carmelite. All have complicated views of practical and doctrinal Christianity especially perplexing to St. Augustine, who, as a pre-Reformation missionary, had never heard of Martin Luther or Protestantism. G.B.S. also set up a reverse Faustus theme. He made it necessary for Augustine to borrow for two weeks an earthly body from one of the three so that he might continue his investigation. The person from whom Augustine borrowed the body would reside in heaven for the two weeks. Humor is provided by the reluctance of the Bishop to accept a two-week sojourn in heaven. Naturally, Shaw placed his characters incongruously and irreverently in relation to Augustine to set up the fun of a religious harlequinade. His taste was scrupulous, however. A parish priest of the old school might well have composed the scenario as far as its theological implications went. Shaw was determined to help Chesterton, not embarrass him.

G.B.S. is on record with a letter that tells the story of the scenario. First, it gives the details of its composition.

CHESTERTON.
SHAW SPEAKS
ATTENTION!

. . . I still think that you could write a useful sort of play if you were started. When I was in Kerry last month I had occasionally a few moments to spare; and it seemed to me quite unendurable that you should be wasting your time writing books about me. . . . When one breathes Irish air, one becomes a practical man. In England I used to say what a pity it was you did not write a play. In Ireland I sat down and began writing a scenario for you. But before I could finish it I had come back to London; and now it is all up with the scenario: in England I can do nothing but talk. I therefore now send you the thing as far as I scribbled it; and I leave you to invent what escapades you please for the hero, and to devise some sensational means of getting him back to heaven again, unless you prefer to end with the millennium in full swing.

Second, in the same letter Shaw made a remarkable offer to remunerate Chesterton for writing the script and to finance production of the play himself. In Shavian fashion, G.B.S. made an elaborate effort to mask his generosity under a welter of business statistics and theatrical jargon involving percentages and copyrights. Third, G.B.S. concluded the letter by making himself available as an active consultant while G.K.C. was writing the play.

For the next few days I shall be at my country quarters, Ayot St. Lawrence, Welwyn, Herts. I have a motor car which could carry me on sufficient provocation as far as Beaconsfield; but I do not know how much time you spend there and how much in Fleet Street. Are you only a week-ender; or has your wise wife taken you properly in hand and committed you to a pastoral life.

Yours ever,

G. Bernard Shaw

P.S. Remember that the play is to be practical (in the common managerial sense) only in respect of its being mechanically possible as a stage production. It is to be neither a likely-to-be-successful play nor a literary lark: it is to be written for the good of all souls.[13]

Shaw's efforts failed to stir Chesterton. He never elaborated upon the scenario. Still, it remains an intriguing result of the literary relationship between the two. When G.B.S.

put himself inside G.K.C.'s head and started to work, he
went a little beyond what one usually credits as good imita-
tion. He proved capable of projecting complex thought pat-
terns so similar to G.K.C.'s as to be remarkable, if not
startling. Years later Shaw would demonstrate the same affin-
ity for G.K.C.'s style as he had for his thought processes. In
1932 G.B.S. would publish for the first time "A Glimpse of
the Domesticity of Franklyn Barnabas," a projected segment
of *Back to Methuselah* which had been dropped from the
play. In "Domesticity" Shaw presented Chesterton as the
character "Immenso Champernoon." Chesterton came alive
so vividly as Champernoon that his wit, epigram, and finally
his character had to be dropped from the script because, as
Shaw admitted, Immenso might have run away with the
whole of *Methuselah* and obscured its original theme. (See
Chapter 6.)

Although his scenario lay untouched, G.B.S. made further attempts to galvanize G.K.C. into action. He still considered playwriting the unifying element in his relationship
with the younger man. More than two years after he had
drafted the scenario, G.B.S. made a last effort to get G.K.C.
to write this particular play. On April 5, 1912 he wrote Mrs.
Chesterton about

> a design of my own which I wish to impart to you first.
> I want to read a play to Gilbert. It began by way of
> being a music-hall sketch; so it is not 3½ hours long
> as usual: I can get through it in an hour and a half. I
> want to insult and taunt and stimulate Gilbert with it.
> It is the sort of thing he could write and ought to write:
> a religious harlequinade. [*Androcles and The Lion*] In
> fact, he could do it better if a sufficient number of pins
> were stuck into him. My proposal is that I read the play
> to him on Sunday (or at the next convenient date),
> and that you fall into transports of admiration of it;
> declare that you can never love a man who cannot write

things like that; and definitely announce that if Gilbert
has not finished a worthy successor to it before the end
of the third week next ensuing, you will go out like the
lady in A Doll's House, and live your own life—whatever that dark threat may mean.[14]

Chesterton did not respond to *Androcles* in the creative
way Shaw had hoped. Yet G.B.S.'s letter to Mrs. Chesterton
was significant. In it G.B.S. specified the sort of drama he
thought G.K.C. should be writing—a religious harlequinade
in the manner of his own *Androcles and The Lion*. The fact
is refreshing. Shaw knew that in such a harlequinade G.K.C.
would present a view of Christianity opposed to his own. In
effect, Shaw was willing to set up a challenger to his own
position. G.B.S. had the grace to welcome challenge especially when an opponent, like Chesterton, had a sense of
humor to complement style, skill, and resource.

Eventually Shaw succeeded. He virtually forced Chesterton to write *Magic* in which G.K.C. pummelled Shaw's
position on everything from religion to vegetarianism. Chesterton even mentioned Shaw by name in *Magic* when he
had the Duke, the maddest of all his characters, conclude a
speech with a typically irrelevant non sequitur: "Modern
man and all that. Wonderful man Bernard Shaw!" No one
laughed louder or praised the play more perceptively than
did G.B.S.

Actually, *Magic* turned out to be a marvelous experience for G.K.C. in every way. Produced by Mr. Kenelm
Foss, the play opened at the Little Theatre in London on
November 7, 1913. The critics acclaimed it first, and when
the public also enjoyed it, *Magic* settled down to a run of
more than one hundred performances. Shaw was so delighted
that he wrote a curtain raiser, *The Music Cure*, for the
hundredth performance of *Magic*. G.B.S.'s curtain raiser,
which played the Little Theatre on January 28, 1914, was

ingeniously contrived to match G.K.C.'s parent work in tone and style. Before the end of 1913 Putnam's Sons had published *Magic* as a book, and it sold well.

Some of the praise for the play emanated from unexpected sources. Certainly novelist-critic George Moore was handing out few accolades in 1913. The author of *Hail and Farewell* was nearing the peak of his phase as a professional acerbic. On top of this G.K.C. had written a negative appraisal of Moore in *Heretics* (1905). Yet on November 24, 1913, Moore felt constrained to write to Forster Bovill:

> I followed the comedy of *Magic* from the first line to the last with interest and appreciation, and I am not exaggerating when I say that I think of all modern plays I like it the best. Mr. Chesterton wished to express an idea and his construction and his dialogue are the best he could have chosen for the expression of that idea: therefore, I look upon the play as practically perfect. The Prologue seems unnecessary, likewise the magician's love for the young lady. That she should love the magician is well enough, but it materialises him a little too much if he returns that love. I would have preferred her to love him more and he to love her less. But this spot, if it be a spot, is a very small one on a spotless surface of excellence.
>
> I hope I can rely upon you to tell Mr. Chesterton how much I appreciated his Play as I should like him to know my artistic sympathies.[15]

Perhaps the most reluctant admirer of *Magic* was Frank Harris. In including a study of Chesterton in his *Contemporary Portraits* (1920) Harris had felt obliged to admit that he was constitutionally incapable of appreciating the type of comic writing in which G.K.C. indulged. For the same reason Harris had never been able to appreciate Aristophanes. Add to this that Harris opposed organized religion in any form, and he becomes almost useful as an antidote to the Roman

Catholic critics of the day who were smothering G.K.C.'s every effort in embarrassing panegyrics. Harris was aware that critics had compared Chesterton's impact on Fleet Street at the turn of the century to that of Samuel Johnson. He would concede only that G.K.C.'s books on Browning (1904) and Dickens (1906) had showed "a certain range of interest" and that his book on Shaw (1909) had given him "position." Just the same *Magic* melted Harris. After citing *The Man Who Was Thursday* (1908) and *Magic* as G.K.C.'s two most "self-revealing books," Harris wrote:

> . . . the heart of him, however, is to be looked for in the noble play, "Magic." I can praise this drama whole-heartedly, because I had again and again coquetted with the idea of writing a tragedy on this same theme.
> I never took up the matter seriously because all the symbols of the mystery are so hackneyed and idiotic; but Chesterton used the chairs that move and the table that tilts and the lights that burn with different colors, and somehow or other the incommunicable is suggested to us and we thrill with the magic of the ineffable; he manifestly rejoices in the fact that there is no ultimate horizon; but visions from the verge that set the unconquerable spirit of man flaming. He at least is a believer, a devout believer, in the Christian faith and Christian dogma. It astonished Carlyle that a man of Dr. Johnson's power of mind and thought in the middle of the sceptical eighteenth century should have been able to worship Sunday after Sunday in the Church of St. Clement Danes. But what would he have said of Chesterton, who, after the theory of evolution has been accepted and Christianity has been studied historically for half a century and is now universally regarded as nothing more than a moment, a flower, if you will, in the growth of the spirit of man, can still go on his knees daily in adoration and still believe like a child in a life to come and a paradise for the true believer![16]

Mrs. Cecil Chesterton, who had spent much of her energy in trying to prove that G.K.C.'s younger brother had been the really important Chesterton, also called a truce when it came to *Magic*. She wrote in 1941: "To this day the play retains dramatic freshness; the conjuror eternally appeals, and the dear old duke, Marie Louise always said he reminded her of Gilbert, has a timeless buoyance. . . . He [Chesterton] found a real delight in writing the play. The mixture of metaphysics and melodrama always appealed to him, and the struggle with the powers of evil gave him considerable joy."[17]

Among G.K.C.'s friends, Maisie Ward noted with humor that all the reviews from Germany compared G.K.C. with Shaw and that some German reviewers thought Chesterton was the better playwright. Miss Ward explained that the Germans could hardly have substantiated G.K.C.'s superiority in the matter of technique. What the German critics meant, either consciously or subconsciously, was that they preferred the ideas of Chesterton to the ideas of Shaw. Miss Ward's personal reaction to *Magic* was on the lyric side. She wrote: "This play is a poem and the greatest character in it is atmosphere. . . . After a passage of many years those who saw it remember the moment when the red lamp turned blue as a felt experience."[18]

The alert Mrs. Cecil Chesterton had picked out protagonist Shaw on opening night: "It was a memorable evening. Gilbert and Frances were almost mobbed in the foyer, and at every interval were eagerly surrounded. . . . When the curtain rang down, Gilbert made one of his wittiest and most delightful speeches . . . Cecil and I foregathered in the bar with Fleet Street critics. Bernard Shaw, I remember, told Gilbert that he had a natural sense of the theatre, and insisted that he must go on writing plays and that a great career as a dramatist lay before him."[19]

Shaw himself was to write the most perceptive criticisms of *Magic*. G.B.S. had the advantage of a tremendous head start in evaluating G.K.C. as dramatist. Some critics were still in the phase of expressing surprise that G.K.C. was able to seem so much at home in a new medium. Others, like Maisie Ward, were noting G.K.C.'s apt use of color or the technical acumen he displayed in achieving such a skillful interweave of characters in the play. All of this was decidedly "old hat" to G.B.S. who from the beginning had sensed all these potentials in G.K.C. True enough, *Magic* had vindicated his superior knowledge of the theatre and superior knowledge of Chesterton, but now G.B.S. was interested in deeper ob-servations on the play. On several occasions Shaw made clear what a high frame of reference he considered appropriate when one was evaluating G.K.C. as a dramatist. Three years after *Magic* had been produced G.B.S. was still capable of writing enthusiastically:

> I agree very heartily with Mr. West as to Mr. Chester-ton's success in his single essay as a playwright. I shirk the theatre so lazily that I have lost the right to call my-self a playgoer; but circumstances led to my seeing *Magic* performed several times and I enjoyed it more and more every time. Mr. Chesterton was born with not only brains enough to see something more in the world than sexual intrigue but with all the essential tricks of the stage at his finger ends; and it was delightful to find the characters which seem so fantastic and even ragdolly (stage characters are usually ragdolly) in his romances became credible and solid behind the footlights just the opposite of what his critics expected.[20]

When G.B.S. wrote the above lines in 1916, the Shaw-Chesterton debating controversy was in full progress. In this particular article G.B.S. was supposed to be making a case "against" Chesterton. Yet once he had touched upon G.K.C.'s ability to create viable character, G.B.S. seemed to forget his original purpose altogether. As he continued to write, he placed G.K.C. in rather exalted company:

> The test [of creating a believable character] is a searching one: an exposure to it of many moving and popular scenes in novels would reveal the fact that they are physically impossible and morally absurd. Mr. Chesterton is in the English tradition of Shakespear and Fielding and Scott and Dickens in which you must grip your character so masterfully that you can play with it in the most extravagant fashion. Until you can present an archbishop wielding a red-hot poker and buttering slides for policemen, and yet becoming more and more essentially episcopal at every roar of laughter, you are not really a master in that tradition. The Duke in *Magic* is much better than Micawber or Mrs. Wilfer, neither of whom can bear the footlights because, like piping bullfinches, they have only one tune whilst the Duke sets everything in the universe to his ridiculous music. That is the Shakespearian touch. Is it grateful to ask for more?

Magic is secure as a solid literary result of the Shaw-Chesterton alliance. And now the references of each man to the other really began to multiply. Even when Chesterton had mentioned Shaw by name in *Magic,* he was not setting a precedent in the burgeoning friendship. Already in 1910 Shaw had mentioned Chesterton by name in his play *Misalliance,* and for good measure G.B.S. had taken a sharp little thrust at G.K.C.'s position on the solidarity of the family in "Parents and Children," the preface to the same play. For almost thirty-five years each would jab affectionately at or exchange compliments with the other—in books, articles, newspapers, prefaces, plays, in whatever writing or speaking media they happened to be employing at the time.

As for *Magic,* only one technical lapse marred its triumph. In the excitement of production Chesterton had forgotten Shaw's stringent advice on finances, had even forgotten to notify his literary agent A. P. Watts, and had sold his manuscript of the play for much less than the proverbial song. Happy as he was about the play, Shaw was on Chesterton like a bearded Irish terrier. "In Sweden where marriage laws are comparatively enlightened," he wrote Mrs. Chesterton, "I believe you could obtain a divorce on the ground that your husband threw away an important part of the provision for your old age for twenty pieces of silver. . . . In future, the moment he has finished a play and the question of disposing of it arises, lock him up and bring the agreement to me. Explanations would be thrown away on him."[21]

A bittersweet quality attaches to *Magic* for it was to be the one and only real play that G.K.C. ever wrote and saw produced and acted out successfully in his own lifetime. Few have ever classified his later stage essay, *The Judgment of Dr. Johnson* (1928) as a genuine drama. More a stage exercise, *Judgment* does, however, have significance for a study of the G.B.S.–G.K.C. playwriting episode. By 1928 for reasons that will be explained, G.K.C. was no longer seriously interested in theatrical technique but the ideas in *Judgment* demonstrated the continuing influence of G.B.S. on Chesterton's mind. At one point G.K.C. even resorted to anachronism to get in a thrust at a Shavian dogma. G.K.C. made the stage Dr. Johnson warn another eighteenth-century character, Mr. John Swallow Swift, not to expect the Superman to emerge in the colonies! After all, says the Johnson-Chesterton character pointedly, democrats like kings are men and not capable of being Supermen.

Unfortunately, G.K.C.'s stage Johnson leaped into full life all too seldom, just often enough for the reader to recognize with a twinge that in G.K.C., Johnson may have been meeting the Englishman best equipped to translate his speech into the dramatic medium. The English theatre has not succeeded to this day in representing the beloved Dr. Johnson accurately on the stage. It would seem that the young Chesterton of 1911, when Shaw was in the wings urging him on, could have done so with ease. All London, including G.B.S., knew that the lumbering Dr. Johnson was the Fleet Street personality with whom the lumbering Chesterton was most often compared. In 1911 G.B.S. had G.K.C.'s mind so stage oriented that Chesterton was thinking in terms of Johnson as a stage character even when he was supposed to be writing straight criticism about him. In that year G.K.C. wrote: "This essential comedy of Johnson's character is one which has never, oddly enough, been put upon the stage. There was in his nature one of the unconscious and even agreeable contradictions loved by the true comedian. It is a contradiction not at all uncommon in men of fertile and forcible minds. I mean a strenuous and sincere belief in convention, combined with a huge and natural inaptitude for observing it."

Then surely because it was 1911 and G.B.S. had his head swirling with ideas for plays, G.K.C. specified precisely which qualities in Johnson would make good material for the stage:

> Somebody might make a really entertaining stage scene out of the inconsistency, while preserving the perfect unity in the character of Johnson. He would have innocently explained that a delicacy towards females is what chiefly separates us from barbarians, with one foot on a lady's skirt and another through her tambour-frame. He would prove that mutual concessions are the charm of city life, while his huge body blocked the traffic of Fleet Street: and he would earnestly demonstrate the sophistry of affecting to ignore small things, with sweeping gestures that left them in fragments all over the drawing-room floor. Yet his preaching was perfectly sincere and very largely right. It was inconsistent with his practices; but it was not inconsistent with his soul, or with the truth of things.[22]

Considering then how well G.K.C. understood the comedy inherent in the character of Johnson, it was particularly unfortunate that his attitude toward the theatre had changed when finally in 1927 he sat down to write, in somewhat rambling fashion, *The Judgment of Dr. Johnson.* By that time G.K.C. had apparently lost the capacity to devote fixed attention or sustained effort to the theatre. In spite of Shaw, his attitude toward it had remained desultory for many years. Even by the time *Magic* had reached the stage in 1913, G.K.C. was experiencing a real life drama which had wrenched him from the theatre and its attractions.

His brother Cecil, through journalistic statements and accusations, had become involved in the Marconi scandals. In a complicated trial Cecil was found guilty of libel and fined but not imprisoned. G.K.C., who had haunted the courtroom, was literally desolate. He had an almost mystic devotion to Cecil which far exceeded the ordinary love of brother for brother. The fact is somewhat odd because the short, stocky Cecil, always pugnacious and crusading, and too often loud, was not the type calculated to rouse mystic devotion in anyone. The adverse outcome of the trial was the immediate reason G.K.C. lost interest in the theatre in 1913. And five years later, in 1918, Cecil died. Immediately G.K.C. deserted, besides the drama, his essays and literary criticism. Clearly his grief was reaching traumatic proportions. Maisie Ward has pointed out that the only overt lie ever attributed to Gilbert Chesterton was his repeated assertion that his brother Cecil had died in combat. G.K.C.'s declaration must have proved embarrassing and induced awkward silences at times. All intimate friends of the two knew that Cecil had actually died of illness in an army hospital.

Unfortunately, when G.K.C. did pick up the pieces of his career, he did so by taking a quixotic plunge into the field of political journalism. He believed that he had necessarily become the spiritual heir to the tasks Cecil had left unfinished. To perpetuate his brother's economic and political theories, G.K.C. assumed multiple journalistic burdens, including the editorship of *The New Witness*. G.K.C. was especially ill-fitted to become an editor. He could scarcely bear to cut the "copy," however banal, of a friend. Incredibly, despite his obvious limitations in the management end, G.K.C. remained in this journalistic morass for a good part of the next twenty years. Shaw was not alone in mourning and, as we shall see later, openly berating what this journalistic episode had done to the rest of G.K.C.'s career.

At any rate the spark of the theatre flared only once more for Chesterton. On that occasion it did flare brilliantly. In 1932, four years before his death, G.K.C. wrote *The Surprise*. It was his third, final, and best play. He had intended that the play should be produced by Miss Patricia Burke. He set it aside for revision, however, never returned to it and, to this day, *The Surprise* has never been acted upon a stage. In fact, the public never saw the play in any form until 1953 when Sheed and Ward published it as a printed play. Since purists insist that a play is not a play at all until it has been performed, one should perhaps control the urge to grow too enthusiastic over *The Surprise*. Yet when Garry Wills examined the printed version he declared that it "ranks with Chesterton's finest creative works—with *Magic, The Man Who Was Thursday, The Wild Knight* and *The White Horse*."[23]

Wills is correct. *Surprise* is not only a powerful display of metaphysical fireworks; it is extremely stageworthy. Set in the same Pyrenees in which mentor Shaw had set his own "Don Juan in Hell" and profiting from generous use of Shavian repartee, the play also has an Elizabethan abundance. Chestertonian swordplay fills the stage. Princes and Princesses enter and exit, always gorgeously appareled, always speaking as Princes and Princesses should speak. Solid ideas spring forth from an intriguing Author-Poet who is very Spanish and very Shakespearian. He controls life-sized puppets who leap to life to perform his play. A colorful old Franciscan Friar "hears" the play as a "confession." Finally, the Author-Poet is a musician, too. The recurrent twang of his guitar lends an extraordinary contemporary touch to the drama.

Had he lived to see it published, G.B.S. would have liked *The Surprise*. Still, the play might have raised the competitive sweat on his brow. At times *The Surprise* rises to Shakespearian heights as well as Shavian. G.K.C.'s insights on the creative process are uniquely presented. His lines illustrating the threat to sanity when the Author-Poet begins to believe that the people he has created are real can rest with dignity just below the lines which begin: "The lunatic the lover, and the poet, / Are of imagination all compact."

Miss Dorothy Sayers has written of *The Surprise:* "Having 'got it out of his mind,' he appears to have set it aside, and done no more about it. Possibly the mere writing satisfied the creative impulse. . . . (It is a pity that he did not write more plays; his gift was naturally dramatic, and *Magic,* slight as it is, has a quality which shows that he could have mastered the technique if he had chosen.)"[24] Miss Sayers seems to have divined the only plausible reason why G.K.C. could have let such a fine play remain unproduced. At least her observations are consistent with the other facts of the last four years of G.K.C.'s life. Rid of his journalistic chores at last, he had returned to his origins, to writing down his primal beliefs on life and art. In that context *The Surprise* was simply a purifying experience for G.K.C. The play contained notions he had to pour out on paper to free his mind of them. Once he had done so, he was content. Actual production of the play would have meant little to G.K.C. Nevertheless, no serious Chestertonian will ever rest content until *The Surprise* gets a hearing on the stage. Yet even if it does get a hearing, and despite *Magic* and *The Judgment of Dr. Johnson,* the Shaw-Chesterton theatre experience must definitely fall into the category of the old poem's lament: "Of all sad words of tongue and pen / The saddest are these 'it might have been.' "

For a fresh analysis of Shaw's critical perception and his true relationship to Chesterton, however, the theatre episode can provide invaluable insights. For example, granting Shaw credit for his solid reputation as a critic, it still remains odd to the point of being uncanny that by 1910 his was the only critical voice raised in London to insist that the theatre was the best vehicle for Chesterton's talents. After all, G.K.C. had never even attempted a play by 1910. The other critics seemed on much safer ground in according G.K.C. a generous niche in other genres in which he had proved himself. Some said his strength lay in poetry. Many critics thought he was best of all in the essay. Others found him most at home in the role of public debater. A growing number of readers were coming to admire him as a novelist or teller of detective tales. None had even hinted that G.K.C. had the potential to be a playwright. Shaw did more than hint. He declared openly that G.K.C. could make an excellent playwright.

Probably Shaw had received his first clue from the similarity to his own methods in the writing methods of the younger man. These similarities had simply been too obvious to be missed by a man of Shaw's critical acumen. The paradox, compression, and epigram, always hailed as cardinal points of G.B.S.'s style, were also cardinal points of G.K.C.'s. Unlike the banal Wildean wits, but like Shaw, G.K.C. was also fast becoming proficient, as Garry Wills has noted, in the technique of *ridentem dicere verum* (in laughing to tell or speak the truth). The comparison holds right down the line. Like G.B.S., G.K.C. was prone to express his thought dialectically. Dialectics imply intellectual conflict, and intellectual conflict was the very stuff of the Shavian approach to the theatre. In composing *Magic* G.K.C. enjoyed most the wrestling in dialogue with the powers of evil, just as Shaw had predicted he would. In many ways G.B.S. was indeed seeing in G.K.C. the exact reversal of his own image in a mirror.

G.B.S. was just as quick to perceive certain basic differences from his own in the Chestertonian technique. When he did, G.B.S. enjoyed the differences and did not try to remake G.K.C. in his own image as some mentors are tempted to do. A case in point was their respective use of symbol. Both men were very much at home in symbolic narrative, but their key symbols differed. Musician Shaw liked to employ music symbolically at climactic points. Artist Chesterton liked to use color. The climactic point in *Magic* came when the red lamp, symbolizing evil, turned blue. G.B.S. was delighted with the scene. Ever after that he insisted that color and art played the same decisive part in G.K.C.'s psychological processes that music did in his own. As he once wrote to Chesterton: "If you can imagine the result of trying to write your spiritual history in complete ignorance of painting, you will get a notion of trying to write mine in ignorance of music."[25]

The resemblances between the men outweighed the differences. Shaw was fitted even by experience to be of specific help to Chesterton. As a frustrated novelist himself, G.B.S. was able to recognize that G.K.C.'s dialogue was all wrong in such novels as his early *The Napoleon of Notting Hill* (1904). G.K.C.'s abrupt dialogue and gesture did seem too thin, too rapid for the more leisurely paced, introspective form of the novel.[26] On the stage, G.B.S. told Chesterton, such repartee and dialogue would be just right. G.B.S. always thought highly of G.K.C.'s ability to create believable human speech. As late as May 17, 1923, Shaw was to put Chesterton among the "elect" as a writer of dialogue: "There is, of course, a born genius for dialogue which needs no training. Moliere, Goldsmith, Chesterton, Lady Gregory are the first highly literary names that occur to me."[27]

G.K.C. displayed another aptitude for the theatre in his delight in suspense and sensational adventure. Garry Wills wrote that Chesterton had a sword and some kind of violence in almost every book he ever wrote, and Wills was intrigued by what that fact might indicate about G.K.C.'s character.[28] Whatever it indicated, G.K.C.'s penchant for violent adventure would have been an asset in the theatre. As Shaw pointed out to everyone, suspense and sensationalism were the very staples of all the great dramatists including Shakespeare. Chesterton had had a delightful time with these ingredients in *Magic*. To heighten effects and meanings G.K.C. had added a conjuror moving in mists on the stage, devils coming alive, and that red light turning blue.

Still *Magic* might have remained superficial drawing room comedy had G.K.C. not borrowed a device from Shaw. G.B.S. had added dimension to his own drawing room comedy *Man and Superman* (1903) by inserting in it a single preternatural segment in which he treated symbolically the Don Juan myth. G.K.C. inserted in *Magic* a preternatural type prologue which had the same effect and was reminiscent of the Shaw scene right down to setting and character. When G.K.C.'s heroine Patricia Carleon appears, she is strolling alone through mists. The Shavian Dona Ana de Ullova makes her entrance wandering alone in mists and void. Patricia has the advantage though of strolling in a garden in which moonlight overrides the mists and she meets fairies, while Ana meets ghosts. Like Ana, however, Patricia must next encounter in her garden a devil figure. Chesterton called his devil figure "The Stranger," and with his cloak and "a pointed hood" he could have moved over to the Shaw tale with ease. Moreover, the Chestertonian "Stranger," like

Shaw's Devil, remained intriguingly ambivalent in his actions. The Stranger wears a sword "but not to slay." Again, he seems much more interested in instructing Patricia in the true meaning of the language of fairies than in menacing her. Such scenes make the reader alert and cannot be dismissed as random interpolations in drawing room comedies. One is forced after such scenes to look for the real meaning of *Magic* and *Man and Superman* far beneath the froth of the "simple" comedies of manners.

Finally, G.K.C. vindicated Shaw's judgment when he succeeded in making the conjuror come alive on the stage. G.B.S. had predicted G.K.C.'s characters would seem more viable on the stage than in any other medium. Actually the conjuror remains the most realistic hero G.K.C. imagined in any genre.

While G.B.S. increased G.K.C.'s artistic scope when he led him to the theatre, he never tried to compromise his individuality. Maisie Ward need not have worried that people would consider G.K.C. only as a Shaw disciple. Miss Ward was upset when as early as G.K.C.'s *Heretics* (1905) a reviewer who could scarcely have read the book classified Chesterton as "a disciple of Shaw." Undoubtedly, Shaw would have scoffed. G.B.S. never tried to "manage" G.K.C. except in matters of finance and in the matter of giving direction to his art, two areas in which the placid Chesterton manifestly needed "managing." G.B.S. had recognized and honored the steel in G.K.C.'s principles immediately. In *Heretics,* G.K.C. had conducted a chapter-long assault on the Shavian spiritual and philosophical breastworks and saved room for a few thrusts at Shaw's political tenets as well.

Such attacks did not ruffle Shaw's insouciance. In fact, he enjoyed such intellectual jousts, especially when they were carried out exuberantly and with intelligence. Shaw had known from 1905, and probably before, that on such ques-

tions as religion he and G.K.C. were inexorably and inalter-
ably opposed. G.B.S. could not care less about *what* G.K.C.
wrote and said. Already, long before 1913, Shaw may be
glimpsed urging Chesterton to write plays along spiritual
lines—anything—just as long as he would write plays. Shaw
was interested in G.K.C. primarily as an artist, not as a disciple. Naturally, however, G.B.S. did not terminate his relationship with G.K.C. precisely at the point of art. He was
humanly conscious of G.K.C. as a man and as a friend
whose thought he understood better than most even when
he disagreed with it.

Most of the occasions on which they met in this period
were quite public. One was for the celebrated mock trial of
John Jasper accused of the murder of Edwin Drood. The
mock trial was a hilarious attempt to solve *The Mystery
of Edwin Drood,* a mystery left unsolved when its creator
Charles Dickens died while his last novel was still very much
in progress. The evidence for the mock trial was heard in
the Kings Hall, Convent Garden, Wednesday, January 7,
1914. The proceedings were to consume four hours and
twenty minutes ending at 11:35 p.m. The trial attracted a
surprisingly large number of the leading political and literary
luminaries of the day. G. K. Chesterton was Judge. Cecil
Chesterton was Counsel for the Defense. Publisher Arthur
Waugh (Evelyn's father) played a witness, one Canon Sep-
timus Crisparkle. Bernard Shaw was elected Foreman of the
Jury. Among his fellow jurors were W. W. Jacobs, Hilaire
Belloc, Max Pemberton, G. G. Street, and William Archer.

The verbatim report of the trial[29] shows that Shaw must
have been as vocal and articulate a Foreman of Jury as has
ever existed. He interrupted the testimony at several key
points, and his contributions were both witty and informed
with insight. Some of his interruptions caused discomfiture
among certain adherents of Dickens who were quite serious

and portentous about this crime "against the peace of every true Dickensian." Mr. Justice Chesterton, however, agreed completely with and concurred heartily in the Shavian approach to the mock trial. G.K.C. did more than accept with equanimity and laughter Shaw's serio-comic speech in which, speaking for all the jurors, G.B.S. directed a verdict of guilty on the head of John Jasper. Judge Chesterton ended the trial in the same spirit with a witty and perceptive speech of his own in which he consigned all present except himself to prison "without any trial whatever!" The Jasper mock trial episode was another instance where G.K.C. and G.B.S. complemented and abetted each other perfectly in public life.

Nevertheless, G.K.C. was not nearly so willing a partner for G.B.S. in their next public encounter which took place six months later on June 6, 1914. Shaw himself described the wild events the next day in a letter to George Cornwallis West, but G.B.S. was never to give the faintest clue as to why the events should have come about in the first place: He had spent the whole day with Chesterton, Archer, and Howard de Walden, Shaw wrote. And they had amazed the local people by running about in cowboy dress, riding over cliffs on bicycles, descending into abysses on ropes, rolling downhill in barrels, wading streams, and other things G.B.S. considered unsuited to his age and dignity. Something similar was apparently planned for the following day but was called off because of bad weather.[30]

As late as 1936 G.K.C. was still mystified by all that bizarre activity. In his *Autobiography* he gave a full and rather fascinating account of what had happened on that June day in 1914. Shaw, in the heartiest of spirits, had knocked on G.K.C.'s door in Beaconsfield and, without preliminary, importuned G.K.C. to join himself, Lord Howard de Walden, and Mr. William Archer, the grave Scottish critic, in acting out the part of cowboys in a film projected by Sir

James Barrie. Flabbergasted at the proposal, Chesterton replied, "after a somewhat blank pause of reflection, 'God forbid that anyone should say I did not see a joke, if William Archer could see it.' Then after a pause I asked, 'But what is the joke?' Shaw replied with hilarious vagueness that nobody knew what the joke was. That was the joke."

Reluctantly, G.K.C. consented to become part of the escapade which divided itself into two parts. First, the four actors met in an abandoned brickfield in the wilds of Essex. There they donned the cowboy costumes, not neglecting to cavil at Archer, who with typical Scottish foresight, had appropriated the best pair of trousers which, trimmed as they were with magnificent fur, made the others seem plain by comparison.

Next, the cameras began to grind away as the four cowboys rolled in barrels, had themselves lowered by rope over fake precipices, and lassoed "wild" ponies so tame that they ran up to the four actors and nosed in their pockets for lumps of sugar. Then all four were mounted on the same motorcycle (G.K.C.'s weight alone putting a strain on the vehicle) as its wheels were spun underneath them to create the illusion that the hardy foursome were hurtling down a mountain pass. Meanwhile the director, Sir James Barrie, hovered about inscrutably, refusing to divulge the purpose of his filmed epic. The assistant director, noted actor Granville Barker, kept shouting at G.K.C. to "Register Self-Sacrifice" or to "Register Resignation," which the hard-pressed G.K.C. managed to do to general applause.

The second half of the adventure took place on the same night. Barrie had arranged a supper meeting at the Savoy Theatre where the four actors could "talk things over" with himself and Barker. Nothing was ever talked over. Instead, when G.K.C. arrived at the Savoy, he found a huge dinner party in progress. Everyone in London seemed to be there from Prime Minister Asquith to an inscrutable Oriental attache. The diners were seated at little tables talking animatedly about everything except the matter at hand as cameras ground away, recording the whole proceedings. When G.K.C. looked at Barrie for an explanation, Sir James only nodded vaguely and continued to pull at his pipe. After dinner the company adjourned to the Savoy auditorium. There, Bernard Shaw, mounted on a stage, harangued the assembly with a furious speech, enhanced by savage gesticulations. At its conclusion, G.B.S. drew an enormous sword. At that signal the other three actors rose in the audience, brandished swords of their own, and pursued Shaw out through the back scenery. And then, as G.K.C. wrote:

> We (whoever We were) disappear for ever from the record and reasonable understanding of mankind; for never from that day to this has the faintest light been thrown on the reasons of our remarkable behaviour. I have since heard in a remote and roundabout way certain vague suggestions, to the effect that there was some symbolical notion of our vanishing from real life and being captured or caught up into the film world of romance; being engaged through all the rest of the play in struggling to fight our way back to reality. Whether this was the idea I have never known for certain; I only know that I received immediately afterwards a friendly and apologetic note from Sir James Barrie, saying that the whole scheme was going to be dropped.[31]

Commenting further on this issue of the cowboy incident, G.K.C. was to make a significant distinction between his relationship with H. G. Wells and his relationship with Shaw in matters of camaraderie:

> In most matters I have found myself rather more in sympathy with Mr. Bernard Shaw than with Mr. H. G. Wells, the other genius of the Fabians, warmly as I admire them both. But, in this matter, Wells was more

of my sort than Shaw. Wells does understand the glow
and body of good spirits, even when they are animal
spirits; and he understands the Saturnalia in which the
senator can sometimes relax like the slave. Even here,
however, there is a distinction. Shaw has plenty of appe-
tite for adventure; but in his case it would be most welcome as open air adventure. He would not see the fun
of cellars or smugglers' caves; but require a levity in
some sense celestial in the literal sense of being *sub divo*.
To put it shortly, Wells would understand larking; but
Shaw would only understand skylarking.[32]

Only on the superficial level of camaraderie could an
H. G. Wells ever be said to have an advantage over G.B.S.
where G.K.C. was concerned. The inner understanding between G.B.S. and G.K.C. was deep and profound. For Shaw
knew the private Chesterton as well as the public Chesterton, just as G.K.C. knew the private Shaw as well as the
public Shaw. It had not been by accident that G.B.S. had
led G.K.C. to the theatre and, in the conjuror, to the most
realistic character he ever drew. G.B.S. knew that Chesterton had been searching to express that kind of reality for a
long time. A public chink opened on the private Chesterton
as recently as 1959, when Evelyn Waugh published for the
first time a letter from G.K.C. to Monsignor Ronald Knox.
The letter caused a stir even among the most knowing Chestertonians who like to preserve his image of constant affa-
bility. In the letter G.K.C. dropped the verbal tricks of his
public person and spoke directly from the heart:

Any public comments on my religious position seem
like a wind from the other side of the world; as if they
were about somebody else—as indeed they are. I am not
troubled about a great fat man who appears on platforms and in caricatures, even when he enjoys controversies on what I believe to be the right side. I am concerned about what has become of a little boy whose

father showed him a toy theatre, and a schoolboy whom
nobody ever heard of, with his brooding on doubts and
dirt and daydreams of crude conscientiousness so incon-
sistent as to [be] near to hypocrisy, and all the morbid
life of the lonely mind of a living person with whom I
have lived. It is that story, that so often came near to
ending badly, that I want to end well.[33]

The private Chesterton of that letter is almost as unknown as is the private Bernard Shaw. For example, the private Shaw corresponded on a plane of genuine delicacy
about his own spiritual position for twenty-six years (1924–
50) with a Benedictine nun, Dame Laurentia of the Stanbrook Abbey. Once G.B.S. even dropped the delicacy to
make plain to Sister the difference between his private and
public concerns. He wrote on July 26, 1946, four days after
his ninetieth birthday:

> Dear Sister Laurentia,
> For the past weekend I have had over 100 congratu-
> lations a day. But for two strong men who have worked
> hard tearing them up for me I should never have been
> 90. Saving your reverence I do not give a damn for con-
> gratulations. But prayers touch me and help me. It is
> good for me to be touched. Stanbrook prayers must have
> some special charm; for I never forget them.[34]

Prayer was to be a recurrent theme in the long correspondence. The letters also revealed an astonishing difference between the public and the private Shaw on the subject
of the Blessed Mother, a figure normally most revered in the
Roman Catholic Church. Publicly, G.B.S. had had occasion
to dispute the miraculous nature of the Virgin Birth and
he never altered his position. Privately, however, G.B.S. revealed in the correspondence that he also had respect for
and devotion to Mary as the Mother of Jesus. On one occasion "Brother Bernard," as he signed himself, quoted scrip-

ture and added a note to assure Sister Laurentia that he had
not forgotten the wishes of the Mother of Jesus; "And Sion
said: Can a mother forget her child, so as not to have pity
on the son of her womb? / When I have to deal with divin-
ity She jogs my elbow at the right moment and whispers
'Now Brother B. dont forget *me*.' and I dont."[35]

The private Shaw of the correspondence with Dame
Laurentia might still seem a stranger to many who thought
they knew Shaw, but he was never a stranger to Chesterton.
G.K.C. knew from the first that spiritual concern was as genuine in G.B.S. as it could possibly be in himself. That fact
only provided a starting point in their relationship. The two
men were to differ sharply on the precise meaning of spirituality, and even more on the means by which spirituality
should be applied to contemporary social life. The differences were to provide much of the material for the marvelous debates and intellectual contests between the two.
Fortunately for the reading public, G.B.S. and G.K.C. were
apparently convinced that magnificent language, the best of
which they were capable, was the proper vehicle for expressing spirit. From the first the relationship led to brilliant writing, some of it already discernible in Shaw's "Chesterbelloc"
essay, the Shavian letters and scenario, and G.K.C.'s *Magic*.

In many key respects, G.K.C.'s book, *George Bernard
Shaw* (1909), was the best early manifestation of the genuine literary accomplishment which the relationship was to
produce. G.K.C.'s study on G.B.S. makes clear that one can
still learn much more about the real Chesterton and the real
Shaw by quietly observing the interaction of the minds of
the two artists, the one upon the other. The book is worth a
chapter all to itself.

two

G.K.C.'S *GEORGE BERNARD SHAW*

All good Chestertonians and Shavians should be thankful that G.K.C. wrote one of the most brilliant books on G.B.S. and that G.B.S. took such violent exception to much that the book contained. The combination of G.K.C.'s solid accomplishment and G.B.S.'s capable rebuttal in book review, letter, and recorded conversation is invaluable for reconstructing the lively controversy between the two men. One could easily conclude that the whole episode was to contain in essence all that was ever to be germane to the G.B.S.–G.K.C. relationship. Such an assertion would be too sweeping mainly because one must look elsewhere for the flamboyance and pithy exchange that normally characterized the public appearances of G.B.S. and G.K.C. Not until 1911 when G.B.S. and G.K.C. mounted the rostrum to debate could one appreciate the unique repartee and dazzle of confusion that lent so much personal warmth to the relationship of the two men. Chesterton and Shaw functioning joyously before a noisy crowd of auditors was also part of the public image they projected for contemporaries.

George Bernard Shaw performed a different function, more permanently valuable, less immediately exciting. The study contained little of the special brand of excitement the men were prone to generate. This was a book about the private Shaw by the private Chesterton. G.K.C. had written a

serious intellectual history of G.B.S. and in the process revealed his own intellectual stance. A strange, almost unreal
quiet falls over the intellectual images of the two men. Was
this the real G.B.S.? Was this the real G.K.C.? Not only did
George Bernard Shaw project the real G.B.S. and the real
G.K.C. but it also provided a valuable cerebral interlude, a
place to view Chesterton and Shaw unimpeded by their char-
ismatic but distracting platform images. Somewhere a clarification should be made on the genuine intellectual positions
of the disputants, and G.K.C.'s book and G.B.S.'s reaction
to it provide exactly this clarification.

Nor does one travel an old road in making a detailed
study of *George Bernard Shaw*. The rise of the book to
critical eminence has been slow and painfully difficult. Not
until 1956 could a Shavian scholar like St. John Ervine
safely put the book into this perspective:

> The number of books about Shaw is already large and
> is likely to be larger. The first biography was the late
> Holbrook Jackson's. It was published in 1907 when
> G.B.S. was 51 and still had a great part of his work to
> do. It has had many followers, including the monumen-
> tal Life by Professor Archibald Henderson, a most use-
> ful quarry for other biographers to dig in, and a char-
> acteristic and brilliant commentary by G. K. Chesterton
> which is the best book on Shaw that has been written
> and will probably be the best that will ever be written.[1]

G.K.C.'s book is proving more useful to contemporary
scholars than it was to scholars in its own day. Various factors had combined in 1909 to divert critical readers from the
book and to obscure its significance. The first culprit was the
general reputation of the two men. *George Bernard Shaw*
was not immune to the exasperating preconceptions that prevented the public from taking seriously any venture involving
both men. Reviewers of the book persisted in declaring that
in reality the points of view of G.B.S. and G.K.C. were prac-

tically identical. Even by 1909 this plaint had grown so hoary that some critics were at least seeking originality of phrase to make the old charge sound interesting. In 1907 one critic had succeeded. He managed to create an imaginative representation of the alleged alter-ego relationship worth reading for its own sake as well as for the point it attempted to make:

> . . . Shaw it is said, tired of Socialism, weary of wearing Jaegers, and broken down by teetotalism and vegetarianism, sought some years ago to escape from them. His adoption, however, of these attitudes had a decided commercial value which he did not think it advisable to prejudice by wholesale surrender. Therefore, in order to taste the forbidden joys of individualistic philosophy, meat, food, and strong drink, Shaw created "Chesterton." This mammoth myth, he decided, should enjoy all the forms of fame which Shaw had to deny himself. Outwardly, he should be Shaw's antithesis. He should be beardless, large in girth, smiling of countenance, and he should be licensed to sell paradoxes, only in essay and novel form, all stage and platform rights, being reserved by Shaw.
>
> To enable the imposition to be safely carried out, Shaw hit on the idea of residence close to the tunnel which connects Adelphi with the Strand. Emerging from his house plain, Jaeger clad, bearded, and saturnine Shaw he entered the tunnel, in a cleft in which was a cellar. Here he donned the Chesterton properties, the immense padding of chest, and so on, the Chesterton sombrero hat and cloak and pince-nez, and he left the Shaw beard and the Shaw clothes, the Shaw expression of countenance, and all the Shaw theories. He emerged into the Strand "G.K.C." in whose identity he visited all the cafés, ate all the meats, rode in all the cabs, and smiled on all the sinners. The day's work done, the Chesterton manuscripts delivered, the proofs read, the bargains driven, the giant figure returned to the tunnel, and once again was back in Adelphi, the Shaw he was when he left it, back to the Jaegers, the beard, the

Socialism, the statistics, and the sardonic letters to the *Times*.[2]

Despite such sprightly comments, the charge that an identity existed between G.B.S. and G.K.C. in the area of philosophical ideas was patently absurd. The two were alike only in that they asked the same pointed questions of society. Their answers to the questions differed sharply. Were it not that in 1909 attack by question alone was enough to make some men uneasy, the charge of an identity of viewpoint between G.B.S. and G.K.C. would actually be incomprehensible. The men were in substantial agreement on only one major issue of the day. Both postulated that the new "religion of science," as they called it, would never provide a general solution for the nation's problems. Otherwise G.B.S. and G.K.C. expressed a dichotomy of viewpoint that could serve as a textbook for a student exploring the age for its polar opposites of opinion. G.B.S. could never accept the old Scriptural Orthodoxy. G.K.C. could never accept the new Agnostic Orthodoxy. Maisie Ward has pointed out that whenever Shaw would say in effect, "Give up pretending you believe in God, for you don't," Chesterton would rejoin, "Rediscover the reason for believing or else the race is lost." Where Shaw said, "Abolish private property which has produced this ghastly poverty," Chesterton would reply, "Abolish this ghastly poverty by restoring property." So it went, and so it would always go when G.B.S. and G.K.C. took up the cudgels.

Reviewers did not encourage the sale of the book to discriminating readers when they insisted on seeing collusion, a kind of identity between G.B.S. and G.K.C. Sophisticated readers, interested in more than an encomium of one man by the other, did not flock to buy or study *George Bernard Shaw*. G.B.S. might well have prevented this situation single-handedly. In 1909 only G.B.S. was aware of what men like

St. John Ervine had come to realize by 1956. G.B.S. alone knew that he had been honestly and brilliantly attacked and honestly and brilliantly praised in *George Bernard Shaw*. Certainly, had he wished to do so, Shaw had the prestige to override the other critics and to gain acceptance for the book by acknowledging the unique power and truth of its insights. *George Bernard Shaw* was the best revelation of the real Shaw that had yet been written and naturally G.B.S. was the only human being alive who could have proved this fact by a simple admission.

For the most human of reasons G.B.S. was simply not yet prepared to accept the book on such terms in 1909. After all, who could reasonably expect a public figure like G.B.S., in the prime of life, to drop his public mask and acknowledge that much of his private self had been revealed, and by his jocular upstart of a protégé, Chesterton, whom he thought would have been better employed writing a play. The scrupulously honest Shaw was in a quandary. Certainly, he did not want to prevent the book from attaining maximum circulation. G.B.S. recognized, by and large with delight, the truth in G.K.C.'s portrait of him. Yet too many of G.K.C.'s insights had hit too close to home. Some of G.K.C.'s praise actually embarrassed G.B.S. in areas where he was shy and modest. Some of G.K.C.'s criticism infuriated G.B.S. in areas where he was vulnerable. Several examples should serve to illustrate the highs and lows of Shaw's problem in dealing properly with G.K.C.'s book. First, even the fact that G.B.S. was capable of being oddly modest or shy was a new concept in 1909 and did not square with the public Shavian image. G.K.C. was not only able to identify such unfamiliar qualities; he was able to explain with ease *why* they existed in Shaw:

> Bernard Shaw has occupied much of his life in trying to elude his followers. . . . This man whom men accuse

of bidding for applause seems to me to shrink even from assent. . . . His critics have accused him of vulgar self-advertisement; in his relation to his followers he seems rather marked with a mad modesty. He . . . wishes to have as few followers as possible. It is partly the mere impatience and irony of the Irishman. It is partly the thought of the Calvinist that the host of God should be thinned rather than thronged. And it is partly, alas, the unhappy progressive . . . trying to destroy his own idol and even to desecrate his own tomb.[3]

Such relatively mild insights represented the lows in Chesterton criticism. G.B.S. could read them calmly, even admiringly, without undue comment. The highs in Chesterton criticism were something else again. For at times G.K.C.'s insights did probe too sharply to the heart of the matter to suit G.B.S. Stung on such occasions, Shaw would lash out at G.K.C. in a manner, that had he prolonged it, would have ended right there his problem as to how to deal with the book and would have stimulated the sales of *George Bernard Shaw* into the bargain. The Shavian vehemence in such instances simply proved beyond doubt that he was taking the Chestertonian allegations seriously. A delightful case in point occurred when G.B.S. sensed instantly that G.K.C.'s banter in his book about the Shavian abstemiousness was only a transparent cover for G.K.C.'s ensuing charge that G.B.S. was a Puritan. Shaw declaimed in print:

Is a man to live on my work and then tell me I was not drunk enough to do it properly? I don't drink beer for two reasons: number one, I don't like it . . . number two: my profession is one that obliges me to keep in critical training, and beer is fatal to training and criticism. . . . Beer drinking is to him [Chesterton] . . . nothing short of the communion. He sees in every public house a temple of the true Catholic faith. . . . Chesterton doth protest too much. . . . I should challenge him to forswear sack and dispute my laurels as a playwright

instead of lazily writing books about me. . . . Have I
survived the cry of Art for Art's sake and War for War's
sake, for which Mr. Chesterton rebukes Whistler and
Mr. Rudyard Kipling, to fall a victim to this maddest of
all cries: the cry of Beer for Beer's Sake?[4]

G.B.S. was not amused. He was convinced that G.K.C.
was becoming too personal. How was a man of his proud
temperament supposed to react to the rather startling revelation that the private Shaw was a Puritan of sorts? Nor was
Shaw's ire misplaced. Shaw scholarship had not noted the
Puritan in Shaw before 1909. It has seldom neglected the
Puritan in Shaw since. G.K.C.'s insight was to haunt G.B.S.
down through the years.

George Bernard Shaw was replete with such original
insights, some flattering, some derogatory, almost all true.
Shaw's quandary increased. Whatever G.K.C.'s limitations
as a biographer or as a literary artist, he apparently had a
genius for insight. The stern integrity in the real Shaw would
not permit him to remain silent. Somehow he had to inform
the public that *George Bernard Shaw* was a major achievement of its kind. Yet, at the same time he did not enjoy the
prospect of admitting that G.K.C. had successfully exposed
and labelled private parts of his mind and soul. How could
he acknowledge G.K.C.'s accomplishment and still throw the
scholars and the curious off the scent of the private Shaw?
The dilemma was difficult, but G.B.S. solved it by writing a
brilliant review which contained an equivocal mixture of
praise and blame for the book. In the review he accorded
G.K.C. full credit for capacity of insight but scored heavily
his deficiencies as a biographer. As G.B.S. wrote suavely at
one point: "Everything about me which Mr. Chesterton had
to divine, he divined miraculously. But everything that he
could have ascertained easily by reading my own plain direc-
tions on the bottle, as it were, remains for him a muddled

and painful problem solved by a comically wrong guess."

Briskly Shaw proceeded to document his charge. He cited "howlers" from G.K.C.'s book including an unfortunate misquotation from *Major Barbara* which led Chesterton to a glaring misinterpretation. Then he ticked off factual errors which had marred G.K.C.'s account—errors about the subject's early life in Ireland, errors about the subject's parents, even errors about the tippling tendencies of the subject's father. For seven-eighths of the famous review G.B.S. so cleverly bedeviled and caviled at Chesterton that one could have forgotten that the other eighth of the review was undiluted praise for a masterpiece of insight. Nor could one fault G.B.S. for making capital of G.K.C.'s factual carelessness. In doing so Shaw breached neither the rules of literary warfare nor the rules of friendship. G.B.S. afterwards made clear in a letter to Maisie Ward that he had made himself personally available for interview by G.K.C. while he was composing the book. He had lived quite close to Chesterton at the time. A simple trip to Adelphi Terrace would have enabled G.K.C. to avoid with ease most of the factual errors. G.K.C. never made the trip. Shaw had legitimate cause for complaint.

Shaw managed to convey the impression in his review that whatever the virtues in *George Bernard Shaw,* the work simply could not serve as a critical index to the Shavian mind or to the Shavian works. Rather, G.B.S. would conclude, G.K.C. was a fine young writer who still had urgent need of the guiding or restraining influence of a Shaw: "For there is endless matter in G.K.C. My last word must be that, gifted as he is, he needs a sane Irishman to look after him."

G.B.S. was to put forth more of this paternal praise-blame persiflage long after he had written his review. He wrote to one of his biographers, Frank Harris, on October 16, 1916, that Chesterton's book was the best of its kind that could be written without actually having read what

Shaw himself had written.[5] Apparently Harris' interest in G.K.C.'s effort persisted, because Shaw wrote him again on January 4, 1918: Chesterton's book was better than Mc-Cabe's even though G.K.C. had evidently never read anything Shaw had written or seen more than one play (which he had forgotten). Chesterton had used Shaw as a peg to support an excellent general essay.[6] G.B.S. was also to deter serious critical examination of *George Bernard Shaw* by another of his biographers, Hesketh Pearson:

> Chesterton's book is a very good one in itself [Shaw told the curious Pearson]. It has little to do with me as G.K.C. has never made any study of my works, and in one place actually illustrates my limitations by telling the world something I should have made one of my characters say in *Major Barbara* if I could have transcended those limitations: the joke being that it is exactly what I did make the character say, as Chesterton might have found had he taken the trouble to open the book (probably he never possessed a copy) and refer to the passage. But if you leave me out of account, you will find, I think, that the book is full of good things, and very generous into the bargain.[7]

Pearson's interest waned. He made no study of the book. For a long time G.B.S. was successful with the same approach. The book was good; it was not about him; where it tried to be about him, it was inaccurate. Many a critic was detoured around it. Archibald Henderson, Shaw's official biographer, scarcely alluded to *George Bernard Shaw*. Even Maisie Ward, Chesterton's biographer, did not account the book one of G.K.C.'s important works. Significantly, the chapter in her *Gilbert Keith Chesterton* (1943), which concerned Shaw-Chesterton materials, was edited for Miss Ward by one Bernard Shaw! Whether by chance or design, *George Bernard Shaw* has achieved status as one of the better keys to the Shavian mind only since the death of G.B.S. Yet even before he went to the literary Valhalla, G.B.S. had had to blurt out in print that *George Bernard Shaw* was a magnificent achievement. In a climactic position in the same famous review, G.B.S. had exclaimed without reservation: "This book is what everybody expected it to be: the best work of literary art I have yet provoked. It is a fascinating portrait study and I am proud to have been the painter's model. It is in the great tradition of literary portraiture: it gives not only the figure, but the epoch. It makes the figure interesting and memorable by giving it the greatness and spaciousness of an epoch; and it makes it attractive by giving it the handsomest and friendliest personal qualities of the painter himself."

Nor did these glowing words of G.B.S. clash with the seven-eighths of the review in which he had caviled at G.K.C.'s factual inaccuracy. It had been a natural move for a seasoned literary campaigner like G.B.S. to hammer away at G.K.C.'s factual inaccuracy in order to provide a smoke screen for his own intellectual privacy. The same seasoned campaigner never forgot for an instant, however, that accuracy alone does not a biographer make. Once G.B.S. lectured Hesketh Pearson like a schoolboy on the same subject. Pearson had communicated to G.B.S. his distress at the number of factual errors in Frank Harris' *Life and Conversations of Oscar Wilde*. G.B.S. was inclined to be lenient in the matter. He told Pearson that he was of the opinion that Harris had managed to create a good portrait of Wilde. Pearson persisted in his criticism, claiming that the book contained many complete fabrications as well as the glaring factual errors. G.B.S. listened patiently but then informed Pearson firmly

> that if a biography showed what manner of man its subject was, it did not matter a straw if every line of it was inaccurate. . . . "It is still, as far as I know, by far the best literary portrait of Oscar in existence. . . .

Sherard [a critic] makes the mistake of thinking that by convicting Frank of inventions and inaccuracies he invalidates the portrait, much as if Millais had painted Oscar in a red tie with a green umbrella. Wilde was never seen with either; but the portrait would be far more truthful than one by a common painter perfectly accurate in every detail."

Pearson shrugged, apparently defeated by G.B.S.'s logic, but then struck a bell with a rueful comment: "I have not noticed that his [Shaw's] attitude is quite the same to a biography of himself."[8] Pearson's dry observation was true of G.B.S. as it would be true of any man. The detached Shaw who gave his blessing to Harris' portrait of Wilde was one person. The involved, personally concerned G.B.S. who fought G.K.C. point by point over the validity of his insights in *George Bernard Shaw* was quite another person.

Actually, except to make clear that a detached G.B.S. always did understand the relative value of factual accuracy in a biography, the subject has little relevance now. Factual accuracy never did have much importance in determining the ultimate fate of a book like *George Bernard Shaw*. For, as G.B.S. knew in the first place, G.K.C. had not written a biography of him and never intended to. Straight biography was simply not G.K.C.'s metier, and he never attempted to write one about G.B.S. or anyone else. What G.K.C. had written was a serious philosophical study of the Shavian mind and the Shavian works. G.K.C. was to employ the same technique in his classic *St. Francis of Assisi* (1923). One does not look into Chesterton for biographical detail about the saint or for the line by line type of appraisal of "Canticle of the Sun." One does look into Chesterton to learn from a genius of insight the mind of St. Francis, the philosophy of St. Francis, and where St. Francis fit into the pattern of Western civilization; "he performed in the fields for the thirteenth century what St. Thomas prepared in the study." One looks into *George Bernard Shaw* for the same reasons, or one does not look at all. Yet G.K.C. does make great demands upon his reader. One must consult an encyclopedia for a short factual account before he can begin to understand G.K.C.'s version of the life of a St. Francis or a St. Thomas Aquinas. One must spend time wading through a Hesketh Pearson or a St. John Ervine for factual data on a Shaw before he can appreciate fully what G.K.C. has written about him.

Again, G.K.C. has been all too vulnerable to literary critics with his sometimes wearying and irritating paradoxes, his notoriously bad grammar, and his uneven, hasty style. His name within the field of the literature he loved too often evokes the condescending smile, the deprecating approach, or perhaps, at best, a random allusion to one of his more quotable lines. Like Shaw he has been accounted in some quarters a literary buffoon, but, unlike Shaw, he never had the defenses or temperament to counter the allegation. But when G.K.C. stepped outside the field of English literature, the quality of his genius became apparent and awesome. Perhaps his most astonishing feat was the masterpiece *St. Thomas Aquinas* written in 1933. Chesterton, who had never attended a university, was neither a trained theologian, philosopher, or hagiographer. The field of Thomistic philosophy alone boasts hair splitters who can make even the more acidulous literary critics look like angels of mercy. Chesterton felt obliged to write an airy little disclaimer in his preface to the book: "This book makes no pretence to be anything but a popular sketch of a great historical character who ought to be more popular. Its aim will be achieved, if it leads those who have hardly even heard of St. Thomas Aquinas to read about him in better books."[9]

G.K.C. need not have troubled to write the disclaimer. His *St. Thomas Aquinas* was to be adjudged the best book ever written about St. Thomas by ranking scholars of the caliber of Jacques Maritain, the scholastic philosopher, Etienne Gilson, the medieval historian-philosopher, and Anton C. Pegis, the theologian. Christopher Hollis has reported the initial reaction to the book: "Thomist scholars were the first and most generous in their praise. Professor Etienne Gilson perhaps the most learned of living Thomists said on reading this book, 'Chesterton makes one despair. I have been studying St. Thomas all my life and I could never have written such a book.' "[10]

G.K.C.'s powers of perception were also evident in his study of G.B.S. Some of his insights in *Bernard Shaw* have already helped to point Shavian scholarship in a positive direction. The most dramatic early instance developed from G.K.C.'s refreshing attitude toward the lengthy Shavian prefaces. Disapproval of the prefaces was still quite general in 1909. First, critics had judged that the prefaces were inordinately long in proportion to the value of what they had to say. G.K.C. disagreed and wrote: "But the truth is that the very rapidity of such a man's mind makes him seem slow in getting to the point. It is positively because he is quick-witted that he is long-winded. A quick eye for ideas may actually make a writer slow in teaching his goal, just as a quick eye for landscapes might make a motorist slow in reaching Brighton."[11]

Second, critics had judged that the prefaces had betrayed G.B.S. into the cardinal dramatic lapse of revealing his moral before he got around to telling his story. G.K.C. maintained that such criticism was irrelevant to a dramatist so complex and original as G.B.S. In a Shavian drama the ordinary short description of the protagonist was not enough. For a Shavian character one must be prepared to understand what certain experiences would mean to that character even before he was told what the experiences were. The point was somewhat difficult to express. G.K.C. had to think hard to find an example to illustrate it. In the process G.K.C. hit upon an inspiration that was not only to solve his problem of expression but was also to provide, as bonus, an excellent plan of organization for his own book *George Bernard Shaw*.

G.K.C.'s "inspiration" was Shaw himself. G.B.S. was the perfect example of a character too complex to understand in terms of his actions alone. Who could possibly write a play or book about the real life G.B.S. without writing a lengthy preface to explain him? One simply could not label G.B.S. an Irishman, a Puritan, and a Progressive and let the statement stand without further clarification. Shaw *was* an Irishman, a Puritan, and a Progressive, but the man was also a genius of such striking originality that he kept spilling over the mold in all three categories. Chesterton, in fact, as he warmed to his task, was to allot a chapter each to G.B.S. as Irishman, Puritan, and Progressive. G.K.C. considered all three chapters prefatory, a necessary background for a serious study of G.B.S. as critic, dramatist, and philosopher. Ironically, G.K.C. had started out merely to put himself on record as a defender of the necessity for the Shavian prefaces. Before he had done with his point, G.K.C. discovered that the entire plan for his own book on Shaw had unfolded, and the work was already three chapters toward completion.

G.K.C.'s plan for his book was sound, and perhaps the best ever devised to get at the essence of the real Shaw. For G.K.C. was correct in asserting that when one called G.B.S. an Irishman, he did not mean just any Irishman. One meant a very special kind of Irishman, an Irishman for whom there was no duplicate. Heredity, environment, and genius had combined to make G.B.S. an Irishman who was both typical and not typical at the same time. G.B.S. was not typical because few Dublin Irishmen were born Protestants as was Shaw. Even fewer were born to the threadbare quasi-aristocratic white-collar class of which his parents were threadbare members in good standing. Later the originality of his theology and the lucrativeness of his plays would also separate G.B.S. from Protestantism and a threadbare white-collar existence much as his birth had separated him from the typical Irishman. G.B.S. was never a typical anything.

On the other hand, G.B.S. possessed two qualities which linked him inexorably with every storybook Roman Catholic Irishman of his period. The two qualities kept G.B.S. forever Irish. The characteristics were "virginity and violence." Every Irishman was proud to possess them in a day when the Irish fought the English at every turn and Ireland could still be called legitimately the Land of the Virgins. Shaw possessed the violence and the virginity in full measure. His very mode of address was pugnacious. G.B.S. started out with the Irish passion to be a nuisance where the English were concerned. He hated many English political, social, and religious dogmas, and was prepared to expend much of his energy and career to slay them. The trait was so Irish that it was even observable in an Irishman like Oscar Wilde who wanted only ease and illusion but always expressed his effete desires in pugnacious and defiant epigrams. G.B.S. was different. Shaw had a doctrine to match the trait, and he was prepared to fight on a magnificent scale. When G.B.S. entered England, some would debate whether he entered as alien, invader, or conqueror. All would be forced to admit that where violence of expression and idea was concerned, he entered England as an Irishman.

Although paradox surrounded the fact, G.B.S. was even more a Green Islander when it came to virginity. G.B.S. could scoff, and he did scoff at the Irish religious reasons for maintaining chastity. Yet G.B.S. himself evinced an ability to maintain a practical chastity on a scale that was awesome to the average Catholic and to the average Irishman. Few Irish artists have ever matched Shaw's delicacy in *John Bull's Other Island,* where he described the horror of the Irish girl at being kissed in the street. G.B.S. was able to write the scene with ease. He possessed the same quality of fastidiousness in his own person. Chesterton, among the awed, went so far as to maintain that G.B.S. possessed the gift which saints have declared to be the peculiar reward of chastity—a clearness of intellect that can only be likened to the clearness of crystal.

If G.B.S. qualified as a unique Irishman, he qualified even more easily as a unique Puritan. When G.K.C. called G.B.S. a Puritan, he meant many things but he did not mean that his friend Shaw was a typical member of the Puritan fraternity. As G.K.C. pointed out, G.B.S. had kept the Puritan conduct but he had dropped the Puritan theology just as he had kept the Christian chastity but reserved the right to ridicule the Christian ethic. Nor was G.K.C. deluded into believing that G.B.S. had become a Puritan in conduct because he happened to have a natural preference for vegetarianism and teetotalism.

G.K.C. maintained that G.B.S. had become a Puritan because of a solid and prosaic fact of history. Puritanism had lingered much longer in Protestant Ireland than it had in such countries as Scotland and England. In the latter two countries nineteenth-century nationalism and its needs had long since swept away most of the effects of the Cromwellian hour in history. In nineteenth-century Ireland such nationalism had originated and spread among Roman Catholics only. Puritanism was strangely insulated and protected as a practicing religion within the tiny faction of Protestants to which Shaw belonged.

G.K.C. was always willing to concede that G.B.S. had come to the habit of Puritan conduct through historical accident and that the Puritan theology had been repugnant to him. Had the Puritan theology appealed to Shaw, G.K.C. could declare, G.B.S. would have been one of the few men alive equipped by nature to fulfill its harsh requirements. The central doctrine of Puritanism demanded concentration on God alone. The true Puritan worshipped in a barn rather than in a cathedral. A barn eliminated the distracting "impediment" of aesthetic beauty. A barn was more conducive to pure concentration on God alone. Nevertheless, the average Puritan had difficulty with pure concentration on a day-to-day basis. Sometimes the average man needed the opportunity to worship with his hands and feet as well as his head. When he was denied the opportunity, the result was often hypocrisy.

G.B.S. was not the average man. G.B.S. could have fulfilled the requirement and not overtaxed his intellectual and ascetic equipment. Added to his negative virtues of abstaining from tobacco, meat, and alcohol, G.B.S. possessed an almost inhuman power of cold concentration. His one problem was that his mind seemed always in a race to outstrip itself, but the problem was solved by his alleviating sense of humor which preserved for him a healthy balance of mind and a contact with ordinary human beings. To Chesterton, for whom meat and ale were integral parts of life itself, one of the more admirable facets of the Shavian modesty was that G.B.S. never fully appreciated the difference in will power between himself and other men. Far from deriding mankind, G.B.S. attributed to men a potential for will power and achievement which their history has all too seldom justified. Long before G.B.S. had postulated that man possessed the potential to become a Superman, he had quietly convinced himself, by his own example, that man could maintain a regimen of conduct such as that practiced by the Puritans. Today the assertion that Shaw had progressed quite naturally from his stance as a disciplined Puritan to his stance as champion of a disciplined Superman seems quite logical. In 1909 the assertion caused a minor furor.

G.K.C. had worked hard to clarify Shaw's early history because not much had been known about G.B.S. as Irishman and Puritan. No such formidable task awaited G.K.C. in explaining Shaw as Progressive. By 1909, G.B.S. had already become firmly established before the British public as that type of progressive known as the Fabian Socialist. Therefore, G.K.C. contented himself for the most part with an analysis of the original techniques G.B.S. employed to promulgate his brand of Socialism. He concluded his segment on Shaw as Socialist by emphasizing the altruistic nature of G.B.S.'s motives for public service:

> The usual mean theory of motives will not cover the case; it is not ambition because he [Shaw] could have been twenty times more prominent as a plausible and popular humorist. . . . Here was a man who could have enjoyed art among the artists, who would have been the wittiest of all the *flaneurs;* who could have made epigrams like diamonds and drunk music like wine. He has instead laboured in a mill of statistics and crammed his mind with all the most dreary and the most filthy details, so that he can argue on the spur of the moment about sewing machines or sewage. . . . Nor will I for one as I pass on to . . . argument or quarrel, neglect to salute a passion so implacable and pure.[12]

In the light of G.B.S. as Irishman, Puritan, and Progressive, G.K.C. was now prepared to evaluate him as critic, dramatist, and philosopher. However, Chesterton was wise enough to avoid the pitfall of trying to cram the wildly original Shaw into any set formula. G.B.S., he insisted, was unique. G.B.S. might be an Irishman, a Puritan, and a Progressive—but not always! As critic G.B.S. was the perfect Wagnerite in music, the perfect Whistlerite in painting, the perfect Ibsenite in drama—but not always. Chesterton did not attempt to fix G.B.S. into a single mold because he relished too much the Shaw whom no rule compassed, the Shaw in whom a touch of mystery lingered.

For example, hardly had the segment on Shaw as critic opened when G.K.C. deviated from his script to speculate that in the realm of music the realistic G.B.S. might be a pure Romantic! He began to look for romantic elements in Shaw's writing as well and found enough to convince him that romantic tendencies were present in the Shavian art and becoming more pronounced as G.B.S.'s career progressed. For Chesterton, *Back to Methuselah* (1921) was to be the work which would culminate the romantic phase that Shaw had begun modestly enough in *Man and Superman* (1901–3). In *Methuselah* Shaw would introduce the Barnabas brothers, a colorful pair of scientific philosophers, who would propose seriously that man by an act of sheer will power could prolong his earthly existence for three hundred years! The insouciant G.B.S., by retaining a skillful rationalistic core in his presentation, was able to make the proposition sound fairly bland and reasonable. Nevertheless, G.K.C. would insist to the end that such an ultimate proposal, no matter what rationalistic claptrap enclosed it, would have been considered wildly romantic in almost any other writer. At the time surprisingly few concurred with G.K.C. Even today the task remains for some scholar to determine definitely, when and how often Shaw slipped over the edge of pragmatic realism into the fantasy world of the romantic. As for Chesterton, he had more than served his function as a pioneer of insight.

Not all of G.K.C.'s flights of insight were so exotic. For the most part G.K.C. did hew closely to his painstakingly evolved criteria on G.B.S. as Irishman, Puritan, and Progressive. Fortunately, his book did not lose sparkle when he did so because G.K.C. knew what was genuinely original in G.B.S. and did not waste time on peripheral or standard Shaw. For example, G.K.C. was one of the first to salute rather than criticize Shaw's famous attack on Shakespeare. G.K.C. recognized that Irishman Shaw had simply been unable to resist assaulting an English institution like Shakespeare, an institution in which even the atheists among the English believed and took comfort. Chesterton wrote: "Moreover, it can honestly be said that Shaw did good by shaking the mere idolatry of Him of Avon. That idolatry was bad for England; it buttressed our perilous self-complacency by making us think that we alone had, not merely a great poet, but the one poet above criticism. It was bad for literature; it made a minute model out of work that was really a hasty and faulty masterpiece."[13]

Actually, G.K.C. made a businesslike and orderly evaluation of G.B.S. as critic and philosopher, besides including in the book a relatively systematic evaluation of each of his plays. The orderly approach might be ranked as the major surprise in *George Bernard Shaw* because an orderly approach certainly was *not* standard Chesterton. In 1935, G.K.C. even added a new chapter "The Later Phases" to the book in order to keep his evaluation of the Shavian plays up to date. Shaw's modest disclaimer that the book was full of good things but not about himself simply did not apply.

Moreover, G.K.C.'s thorough knowledge of Shaw's philosophy led him again and again to original and stimulating comments on G.B.S.'s literary style, a technical area of contribution to Shaw study for which Chesterton has seldom been given sufficient credit. A prime instance involved G.K.C.'s concept of the role that characterization played in a Shavian drama. G.B.S. had always been described as a modern writer of "problem plays." G.K.C. objected. The tag did not fit neatly. *Hamlet* was a problem play. Shakespeare

left questions unanswered about Hamlet. Shaw had a different style. He left no questions unanswered about a major
character. One knew precisely where John Tanner stood in
Superman and one knew precisely where the Brothers Barnabas stood in *Methuselah*. Certitude was a virtue for G.B.S.
in public life where he had the courage and the knowledge
to answer every question asked of him. In literary life, however, such certitude about a character was an artistic evil
rather than an artistic virtue. Character, or at least a sense
of mystery and enchantment in the characterization, always
suffered in Shaw.

G.K.C.'s insight initiated a controversy, as yet unre-
solved, over the success or failure of Shavian characterization. Today more critics do tend to agree with G.K.C.'s side
of the question. Shavian scholar Eric Bentley is convinced
that Shaw's "all inclusiveness" in character has deprived
audiences of the opportunity to exercise their imaginations,
normally an integral and exciting part of playgoing. When
G.B.S. had finished delineating a character, there was no
room left to invest that character with some mystical or
mythic past. One knew all there was to know. In 1964, Dr.
H. M. Geduld made an explicit study of the characterization
in *Back to Methuselah*. His conclusions also seemed to support G.K.C.'s original theory:

> This cuts to the very heart of the perennial controversy
> over Shaw's characterization: Has Shaw created char-
> acters or merely Shavian "mouthpieces"? Are we con-
> fronted with puppets motivated by a theory of human
> society applied to dramatic characterization? . . . In
> effect the issues of a Shaw play will determine the range
> of character. . . . Shaw has no wasted elements of char-
> acterization—every detail, every trait is relevant to the
> most direct exposition or to the most exhaustive dis-
> quisition. This frequently produces the strong Shavian
> character who lives within the play but not beyond it.[14]

A second prime instance of Chesterton commenting on Shaw's literary style involved the subject of paradox as a literary device. Critics and public had often attached the label "paradox" to Shaw's literary method. Once more G.K.C. objected. He maintained that G.B.S.'s cast of mind was not in the least paradoxical. In paradox the inconsistency expressed was only apparent inconsistency. Every perceptive person knew what Christ really meant when he said, "He that shall lose his life, the same shall save it." No actual contradiction was involved if one believed in Christianity.

Shaw's basic method was the exact opposite to paradox. Consistency was the Shaw motif, not inconsistency. Often the consistency was mad; often the consistency was wild, but always it was consistency. A man might propose that the principle of complete freedom of thought should be preserved in the education of the young. Shaw would express his objection to the principle by stretching it to more absurd lengths than it had ever been stretched before. G.B.S. would establish first that to preserve such a principle a child should never be taught one course of action unless he was also taught its opposite. If a child struck his mentally retarded sister a sharp blow on the temple, he might be chastized. On the other hand a Nietzschean disciple must also be present to instruct the boy that he might well have struck a blow to insure that the unfit be removed from the world. A little girl might be advised legitimately that it was dangerous to drink from a bottle labelled "Poison" but only if a Christian Scientist were present to apprise her of the view that the poison could not harm her without her own consent. The imaginative Shaw could extend such a gambit *ad infinitum*. Along the way, irony, sarcasm, a dash of invective, much humor—all would come into play to enliven the Shavian text. But no paradox was involved. No contradiction was present. G.B.S.

had carried the one principle of free thought to absurd but logical extremes. Consistency still ruled.

Chesterton admired the method. He acknowledged that by means of it Shaw had performed fine intellectual work in the purification of areas of thought that had become clouded. At the same time the public would have benefited had it realized that Shaw's dialectics involved no contradictions or paradox. To have understood the Shavian motif of consistency would have helped to clear away much confusion concerning the Shavian pronouncements. The public might have grasped more quickly that the creator of the Barnabas brothers really did believe that life spans of three hundred years were a literal possibility.

Sometimes, because of the very philosophical differences between the two, one may encounter in Chesterton insights on Shaw not available anywhere else. The disagreements seemed to clear the air for a better understanding. One must guard against deducing from these healthy disagreements between G.B.S. and G.K.C. a transcendent boon for which Shaw scholarship was in sore need. Fortunately, Shaw has never suffered unduly from servile treatment. The biographer-critics already mentioned, such as Henderson (official), Ervine, and Pearson, were perfectly willing to disagree with G.B.S. and each did differ with him sharply at times. Nevertheless, these biographer-critics did leave room for G.K.C. to do valuable original work. Their disagreements with G.B.S. were usually peripheral because all three men were basically Shavians. G.K.C. was not. In that fact still lies the key to why G.K.C. wrote the most stimulating of all studies of G.B.S. As G.K.C. put it frankly: "Most people either say that they agree with Bernard Shaw or that they do not understand him. I am the only person who understands him, and I do not agree with him."[15]

He had a point. G.K.C. understood G.B.S. as perhaps no man had previously. Part of his understanding included knowledge of the superb virtues of the man, his overriding compassion and sincerity. One result of his total understanding was that G.K.C. was able to keep his criticisms controlled and objective. The man was not prepared to dilute his admiration for Shaw with petty carping.

Nor should it any longer shock or surprise that G.K.C. who devoted studies to saints like Thomas and Francis also devoted a study to an apparent heretic like Shaw. G.K.C. was never more consistent. From the first he attributed to Shaw a nobility in body and spirit that he called Christlike. In 1906 Rodin, the sculptor, had noted a purely physical resemblance between G.B.S. and the traditional Christ figure. Chesterton marked the physical resemblance but he was also prepared to liken Shaw to Christ in spirit. One must go far to encounter more beautiful or provocative lines on G.B.S. than these:

> There exists by accident an early and beardless portrait of him which really suggests in the severity and purity of its lines some of the early ascetic pictures of the beardless Christ. However he may shout profanities or seek to shatter the shrines, there is always something about him which suggests that in a sweeter and more solid civilization he would have been a great saint of a sternly ascetic, perhaps of a sternly negative type. But he has this strange note of the saint in him; that he is literally unworldly. Worldliness has no human magic for him; he is not bewitched by rank nor drawn on by conviviality at all. . . . All the virtues he has are heroic virtues. Shaw is like the Venus de Milo; all that there is of him is admirable.[16]

G.K.C.'s original view of Shaw as a Christ figure has always attracted notice but not always agreement. His book contains dozens of insights capable of causing the same reaction. *George Bernard Shaw* may be many things, good or bad, according to the special point of view of its reader. More than a half century after its publication the book does remain a stimulating and unique accomplishment, an entry of permanent value in the bibliography of Shaw scholarship.

three

GENESIS OF "THE DEBATERS OF THE CENTURY"

When G. K. Chesterton debated Bernard Shaw for the first time in 1911, the event constituted a climax in the career of the rising young journalist. Yet all the years between 1901 and 1911 had been good years for G.K.C. In 1901, armed with swordstick, arrayed in cape and slouch hat, Chesterton had seemed to spring full blown out of nowhere to capture Fleet Street as it seldom had been captured since the days of Samuel Johnson. Suddenly he was writing articles for *The Speaker* and was contributing weekly features, poems, and reviews to the *Daily News*. Within a year he had gained recognition as one of the leading radical political journalists and he was lecturing and debating everywhere. Robert Blatchford, editor of the radical *Clarion* and defender of Atheism, wondered out loud how he had become totally embroiled in debate with a man not yet thirty years old. Bernard Shaw did not waste a moment on such speculation. He let it be known quickly that even before the two men had met on a platform, G.K.C. was already his favorite foe. Still, it had been G.K.C.'s debate with the well-known Blatchford that had propelled him to instant fame as a controversialist.

Simultaneously, G.K.C. was gaining a reputation in every Fleet Street pub as a kindly jester, a man who had a word and a joke for everyone. On Fleet Street when asked what single book he would want in his possession if stranded on a desert island, G.K.C. had replied without breaking stride, *"Robertson's Guide to Practical Ship Building."* To a cab driver who suggested that he try to get his enormous girth into a cab by going sideways, he announced, "I have no sideways." Even the quiet and refined Frances Chesterton, his bride of June 28, 1901, had inadvertently added to the legends growing about G.K.C. When her husband had gained weight as fast as he was gaining fame, Frances despaired of making him look handsome but determined to try to make him look picturesque. Therefore, she had designed the famous cape and slouch hat and innocently provided caricaturists of the day an immediate signature with which to identify G.K.C. On the other hand, the swordstick he affected was G.K.C.'s own choice, a bit of pure Chesterton. G.K.C. had come to enjoy slashing away at flowers or imaginary enemies with the sword cane. More than a little evidence suggests that the flamboyant G.K.C. of 1901 was reacting sharply to a rather solemn boyhood and to a rather serious case of solipsism, which he had suffered during his term as an art student at the Slade School. The early Chesterton of 1874–1900 never became generally known to the British public.

In the same years between 1901 and 1911, the more reserved and poetic Chesterton was also attracting to himself a growing coterie. In 1900 his first two books, *Graybeards at Play* and *The Wild Knight and Other Poems*, had appeared. Twenty-two more books were to spill from G.K.C.'s prolific pen between 1901 and 1911. Among them were: *Twelve Types, Robert Browning, The Napoleon of Notting Hill, Heretics, Orthodoxy, George Bernard Shaw, The Man Who Was Thursday,* and *The Innocence of Father Brown.*

Bernard Shaw watched with delight as Chesterton emerged to fame on Fleet Street. G.B.S. enjoyed the flamboyant side of Chesterton but he recognized at once that

G.K.C. was essentially a serious man. Shaw knew all too well that the humorist can never expect the public to take him as seriously as he might wish even when he is speaking on serious matters. Therefore, G.B.S. took pains to make clear that when he began to call Chesterton a man of "colossal genius" he was not speaking of a cheerful fool who made black and white judgments and scattered little nuggets of Norman Vincent Peale's *Positive Thinking* along the way. Rather, G.B.S. was speaking of a man who exhibited at all times in his judgments what G.K.C. himself had called "a reverent agnosticism toward the complexity of the human soul."

Aside from his general admiration for Chesterton, aside from the counsel he was able to afford him as playwright, Shaw welcomed G.K.C. as a godsend in another area. G.B.S. was badly in need of a first-class debating opponent. By 1911 G.B.S. had lectured and debated on at least one thousand recorded occasions.[1] He had achieved such awesome proficiency that later he would describe his speaking ability as analogous to the pugilistic ability of his friend Gene Tunney, the heavyweight champion. Tunney had declared it criminal for a professional fighter to engage a layman in fisticuffs, and G.B.S. was to write: "I never challenged anyone to debate publicly with me. It seemed an unfair practice for a seasoned public speaker to challenge a comparative novice to a duel with tongues, of no more value than any other sort of duel."[2]

All the same Shaw loved to debate and by 1911 he actually was in the market for a new and talented volunteer to do battle with him. Men of the caliber of H. G. Wells and Hilaire Belloc could often give G.B.S. a spirited contest on paper but never on the platform. Fortunately, Chesterton was to prove an exception. In fact G.K.C.'s skill as a debater was to grow so comparable to Shaw's that he too ran out of other opponents who could match wits with him. For example, the American lawyer Clarence Darrow enjoyed a good and deserved reputation as a debater, but whenever he clashed with Chesterton on a platform, G.K.C.'s incisive mind and superior repartee could reduce him to helplessness within a matter of moments. Mr. Joseph Reilly attended one such debate between Darrow and G.K.C. where the results were measurable. When the two had finished arguing the story of creation as presented in Genesis, slips of paper had been passed out so that each member of the audience could express an opinion as to who had won the debate. The award went overwhelmingly to Chesterton. Mr. Reilly reported: "Darrow in comparison, seemed heavy, uninspired, slow of mind, while G.K.C. was joyous, sparkling and witty. . . . The affair was like a race between a lumbering sailing vessel and a modern steamer."[3]

Another witness to the same debate, Mrs. Frances Taylor Patterson, was even more emphatic. When she had returned home from the debate which took place before an overflowing crowd at the Mecca Temple in New York City, Mrs. Patterson wrote: "I have never heard Mr. Darrow alone, but taken relatively, when that relativity is to Chesterton, he appears positively muddle-headed." Cyril Clemens reported on the same episode: "Although the terms of the debate were determined at the outset, Darrow either could not or would not stick to the definitions, but kept going off at illogical tangents and becoming choleric over points that were not in dispute. . . . Whatever brilliance Darrow had in his own right, it was completely eclipsed. . . . Chesterton had the audience with him from the start, and when it was over, everyone just sat there, not wishing to leave. They were loath to let the light die!"[4]

Yet G.K.C. did not enjoy such unequal contests on the platform any more than did Shaw. Most often, the gentlemanly Chesterton could be found glossing over his opponent's lapses by making jokes about his own ineptitudes. Apparently G.K.C. did succeed in ending his controversies with Darrow on a graceful note. For shortly before his death Clarence Darrow, who had argued so nobly with William Jennings Bryan on the issue of evolution, wrote to Cyril Clemens: "I was favorably impressed by, warmly attached to, G. K. Chesterton. I enjoyed my debates with him, and I found him a man of culture and fine sensibilities. If he and I had lived where we could have become better acquainted, eventually we would have ceased to debate, I firmly believe."[5]

On the other hand, all seem to agree that Bernard Shaw and G. K. Chesterton were always well matched as debaters. On a given night G.B.S. might defeat G.K.C. On another G.K.C. might defeat G.B.S. No one else seemed able to defeat either. Perhaps, after all, G.B.S. and G.K.C. were fated literally to be what Hesketh Pearson dubbed them: "Debaters of the Century."

It seemed inevitable from the first that G.B.S. and G.K.C. would become ideal foes on paper and on platform. Garry Wills has written: "Many saw a resemblance in compression, paradox, and epigram between the established dramatist and the rising journalist. What is more important, Shaw and Chesterton were fascinated with each other, as their voluminous descriptions of each other indicate. . . . Shaw's importance among the Fabians and the Fabians' importance in this century have proved Chesterton wise in the choice of a foe."[6]

Shaw biographer St. John Ervine put the matter even more explicitly: "Mr. Chesterton was sent into the world by an all just God, for the exclusive purpose of saying the opposite to Mr. Shaw. With the most complimentary intention I say that Mr. Chesterton's job in the world is, when Mr. Shaw speaks, to reply, 'On the contrary!' . . . He has to restore the balance which Mr. Shaw very vigorously disturbs."[7]

Critics agree that the stage was beautifully set for public encounter between G.B.S. and G.K.C. Nor were the two ever to haggle over minutiae in the choice of subjects for debate. The issues were always to be defined by the contestants with a whimsical and plastic looseness so that ample room was left for the delights of digression and the exercise of wit and ingenuity. When G.K.C. and G.B.S. mounted a rostrum to debate, religion or some aspect of Shaw's Socialism and Chesterton's Distributism were sure to enter into account along the way. Besides these staples, G.B.S. and G.K.C. between them were prepared to debate most subjects under the sun or over the moon. The format was as simple and as exciting as that.

Nevertheless one must not expect too much of the Shaw-Chesterton debates today. Time has managed to spread its inevitable mists over them. When the debates are read, the repartee does not seem to sparkle quite as it did for its contemporary audiences. Old issues cool fast. Chesterton's Distributism has become passé as a social doctrine. Shaw's Socialism does not generate the excitement it once did, although G.B.S.'s place in history as a champion of Fabian Socialism remains secure. Oddly, history seems to be rendering an opposite verdict on the contribution of the two men to religious speculation. Shaw's Life-Force theory seems to have lost much of its sheen, especially in the debates where it is divorced from the fictional characters who made it attractive in the plays. G.K.C.'s attitude toward religious issues which during the debates worried Belloc ("he gets on too well with the enemy") is now considered very advanced, a clear adumbration of the ecumenical dialogue so popular today in religious circles.

Fortunately time ceases to be a negative factor once it has been acknowledged that the passing years have diminished the fresh impact of the debates, and that the heat has gone out of the issues which so stirred the original auditors. Today one can judge the debates much more objectively. Even more than most famous debaters, G.B.S. and G.K.C. possessed such distinct personalities and held such distinct views that no half-way house was open to the contemporaries who appraised them. Everyone who attended a Shaw-Chesterton debate seemed to be solidly pro-Shaw or pro-Chesterton so that audiences quickly fell into opposite and subjective camps. For example, Shavians like St. John Ervine and Hesketh Pearson were inclined to award the palm of victory to G.B.S. in all of the debates while Chestertonians W. R. Titterton, Desmond Gleeson, and Maisie Ward postulated that debates were decided by the quality of the repartee and that, at repartee, Chesterton was unbeatable. Frank Swinnerton's experience suggests that winner and loser were most often decided on ideological rather than rhetorical grounds:

> I first began to read Gilbert Chesterton's books when I was about sixteen; and this was because I began at that time to work in the same business as another youth, rather older than myself, whose favourite author Chesterton was. . . . We also went to hear Chesterton lecture and debate. But in those days I was a Shavian, which meant that I took the Shavian part in our own discussions, and was forced by my opinions to attack those of my friend (and Chesterton); so that while the admiration I felt for the great man whose loss we mourn was sincere, it was tempered by inability to accept his views of life and death.[8]

Unfortunately, although a Shaw-Chesterton debate is reprinted occasionally, one never finds more than one in the same book so that it is difficult to study the debates in relation to one another. No one maintains that such old debates on such old issues are of major importance in themselves. Nevertheless, two major artists developed and refined attitudes and stances which led to much of what was to be great and permanently attractive in their books and plays. To prove this assertion one need go no further than Shaw's address "The Religion of the Future," which G.B.S. delivered in 1911 and which was to be the very first Shavian statement that G.K.C. rebutted publicly. G.B.S. had more or less outlined his religious position in several plays, notably *Man and Superman* (1903), but "The Religion of the Future" and G.K.C.'s reply to it provided an almost exact blueprint for his theological statements in *Back to Methuselah* (1921). Lest anyone miss the connection or underestimate the Chestertonian influence on Shavian ideas, Shaw even put G.K.C. as the character Immenso Champernoon into a projected segment of *Methuselah*. In the play Immenso performed much the same function G.K.C. had performed in real life in debating G.B.S. on "The Religion of the Future."

Although such exotic literary values are inherent in the Shaw-Chesterton debates, a more humble task remains to be performed before one can look into them. Many of the debates were not recorded, and many have faded from the keenest memories of the people still alive who were fortunate enough to listen to them in person. Therefore, the first order of business would seem to be to collect what is left to be collected of the famous verbal encounters. At least three of the formal debates and one of the informal conversational debates can still be resurrected, almost verbatim, from newspaper accounts, pamphlets, and books. The facts of the G.B.S.–G.K.C. encounters, put into focus in one place for the first time, should allow a more meaningful analysis of the debates in relation to one another and in relation to the respective careers of Shaw and Chesterton.

four

THE FIRST PUBLIC ENCOUNTERS

To get at what transpired and what was said, and under what circumstances, is not always easy when it comes to giving a factual report and evaluation of a Shaw-Chesterton debate. As late as 1958, for example, Mr. Vincent Brome left a misleading impression in his book *Six Studies In Quarreling* as to what actually happened in the first debate between G.B.S. and G.K.C. Obviously Brome, an admirer of the whole era as well as of Shaw and Chesterton, was only trying to entertain rather than to mislead when he reported that "the first big public 'debate' between them in person took place in Cambridge in 1911, when Shaw and Chesterton addressed the Heretics [Club]."[1] Then the author proceeded to give a lively account of the "debate" on "The Future of Religion"[2] in which he juxtaposed Shaw's statements on religion and Chesterton's replies so ingeniously that unless one paid the most scrupulous attention to certain of the footnotes, he might easily have been convinced that an in-person debate was really going on and that Bernard Shaw had delivered a brilliant main speech, but, strangely mute in his own defense, had been soundly thrashed by Chesterton in rebuttal.

Nothing could be less fair to Shaw or even, ultimately, to Chesterton. For Bernard Shaw was all alone, the only speaker on the platform, when he made his address on "The Future of Religion" to the Heretics in the Victoria Assembly Rooms,

Cambridge, on Monday evening, May 29, 1911. Similarly, G. K. Chesterton was the only speaker on the platform when he made his address "Reply to Mr. Shaw on The Future of Religion," also to the Heretics but delivered almost six full months later on Friday evening, November 17, 1911, and delivered in a different setting, the Guildhall, Cambridge!

Further, Shaw had no way of knowing on that Monday evening in May as he strode purposefully to the speaker's platform that the Heretics were soon to invite Chesterton to rebut his speech publicly at a later date. G.B.S. would not have quailed at the fact, but it is probable that he would have prepared his speech along different lines, especially one mystic portion which does not lend itself to logical debate or to logical rebuttal at all. Finally, Shaw had none of that psychological stimulation which applies immediately when an opponent is seated in another corner of the platform ready to seize on one's every remark. Likewise, Chesterton was to give a workmanlike "Reply" to Shaw on a brisk November evening that hinted of snow but he, as much as G.B.S., missed the stimulating presence of a live opponent. For G.K.C. was ordinarily not very good at composing or delivering main speeches although he shone in the give-and-take, repartee sections of a debate. Therefore, in the ordinary sense, the first debate between G.B.S. and G.K.C. was not a debate at all. Nevertheless, the speeches of the two men did constitute the first public oral contest between them, and as such must be reported scrupulously because the contest contained genuinely significant elements.

First, in "The Future of Religion" Shaw urbanely proclaimed that God had died in the nineteenth century, therefore stating more than a half century ago the "God Is Dead" theory which even today is capable of commanding headlines when debated by priests, theologians, and philosophers. Unfortunately, today's priests, theologians, and philosophers often handle the subject so ineptly and superficially in comparison to G.B.S. that to reread "The Future of Religion" and Shaw's other religious speeches is to consult a textbook primer on how far the art of oratory and persuasion has declined. Second, Chesterton in his "Reply" also was about half a century in advance of his times when he avoided all of today's hand-wringing, agonizing answers to the proposition that "God Is Dead" but chose instead to answer the master on the facetious level.

G.K.C. began by laughingly pointing out to G.B.S. that certainly God had died in England in the nineteenth century but actually God had died many times before, had died in fact in parts of the Middle Ages, in the Renaissance, and in the eighteenth century, and G.K.C. wound up by challenging his friend Shaw to solve the much more difficult and interesting problem of how in hell or heaven God had managed to come back to life so many times. In so doing G.K.C. pinpointed the immense sanity of the Shaw-Chesterton oral contests, the fact that two civilized men could argue such a solemn proposition as the death of God and still leave themselves and the audience secure in the knowledge that, whichever side was right, the sun would still come up the next morning and shine on the efforts of a humankind struggling for truth. Best of all, although Shaw thought God was dead, he was not complaining about the fact in existential despair but rather was very hard at work manufacturing and promulgating for the twentieth century his own new God of the Life-Force. On the basis of the "God is Dead" contest alone, Shaw's speech on "The Future of Religion" and G.K.C.'s "Reply" retain intrinsic merit and deserve rereading for more than the usual reasons of historical and scholarly interest.

Besides, the contest did alert Shaw finally to G.K.C.'s capabilities as well as potential as an opponent; it also taught G.K.C. that a major address by Bernard Shaw was almost, if not quite, irrefutable; finally, and perhaps most important, Chesterton's sane reaction and good humor in dealing with the religious "heresies" in Shaw's speech, in contrast to the insane ravings of the newspapers of the day, demonstrated that G.B.S. had great need for a judicious and objective opponent of the caliber of G.K.C.

Chesterton understood three qualities in Shaw as a lecturer, all to be exhibited by G.B.S. in "The Future of Religion," that enabled G.K.C. to debate him on terms that no other man alive was capable of because only the first of the three qualities was generally understood by other men. Even concerning the generally understood quality, that is, Shaw's physical presence, voice, gesture, and rapport with an audience, G.K.C. was more eloquent and accurate than most:

> The first fact that one realises about Shaw (independent of all one has read and often contradicting it) is his voice. Primarily it is the voice of an Irishman, and then something of the voice of a musician. It possibly explains much of his career; a man may be permitted to say so many impudent things with so pleasant an intonation. But the voice is not only Irish and agreeable, it is also frank and as it were inviting conference. This goes with a style and gesture which can only be described as at once very casual and very emphatic. He assumes that bodily supremacy which goes with oratory, but he assumes it with almost ostentatious carelessness; he throws back the head, but loosely and laughingly. He is at once swaggering and yet shrugging his shoulders, as if to drop from them the mantle of the orator which he has confidently assumed. Lastly, no man ever used voice or gesture better for the purpose of expressing certainty; no man can say "I tell Mr. Jones he is totally wrong" with more air of unforced and even casual conviction.[3]

Perhaps it was Shaw's studied casualness that caused the public to miss in large part a second quality that G.K.C. dis-

cerned in him as lecturer and debater. Chesterton knew that
G.B.S. put as much energy and skill into a speech as his
genius was capable of producing. He earned a living from
the inkpot, but his heart was on the platform. Shaw had once
flared up at one of his biographers, Henry Charles Duffin:
"You think of me only as a playwright. Yet for every play
I have written, I have made hundreds of speeches. Your last
section . . . is wrong all through. I never 'realized the futility
of talking to empty pews'; the pews were never empty. . . .
You evidently have not followed my work as a Socialist; and
you had better keep clear of it, unless you are prepared to
make a study of it, which will take you a long time."[4]

Shaw would never have to flare up at G.K.C. on points
like this because Chesterton understood the platform G.B.S.
too well. Once when G.K.C. found it necessary to turn from
Shaw's Socialism to appraise his dramas, he warned his
readers quickly: "I propose here to dismiss this aspect of
Shaw; only let it be remembered, once and for all, that I am
here dismissing the most important aspect of Shaw. It is as
if one dismissed the sculpture of Michael Angelo and went
on to his sonnets. . . . Socialism is the noblest thing for
Bernard Shaw; and it is the noblest thing in him."[5]

Chesterton was all alone in recognizing a third quality
in Shaw as debater and lecturer, and it was this quality which
was to be of the most specific help to G.K.C. in dealing with
G.B.S.'s speech on "The Future of Religion." The critical
insight that provided G.K.C. a genuine advantage over other
critics was—according to J. Percy Smith—"that he was the
first, and remains one of the few to see this truth about Shaw
and take it seriously: that he had experienced religious
conversion."[6]

When Shaw spoke as a mystic on "The Future of Religion," the orthodox Chesterton took him seriously. Ironically,
the unorthodox Heretics did not but rather guffawed in all

the wrong places. The Heretics were positive that, by definition, Bernard Shaw was their spiritual brother, a man who shared all of their views on what should happen to religion in any form. Old G.B.S. was to them an atheist, if anything, and partly because of this and partly because of the nature of a frolicsome college crowd on a balmy May evening, the Heretics accorded Shaw a standing ovation as he mounted the rostrum in the Victoria Assembly Rooms. The fact that G.B.S. was obviously in a brisk and serious mood and prepared to deliver a succinct and definitive view of his religious position did not dent the festive attitude of the Heretics and they continued to cheer and laugh long after G.B.S. was ready to begin. True to Shaw's remarks to biographer Duffin on his abilities as a crowd puller, the hall had filled long before G.B.S. arrived and now the walls were lined with standing students, and a crowd was beginning to assemble in the streets outside the lecture rooms. More than a thousand people were present. Finally, G.B.S. himself signalled to F. M. Cornford, the chairman, to begin the proceedings. That august individual did still the crowd but he was not inclined to hurry his introduction. The scholarly Cornford was himself a daring heretic by the gentle Cambridge standards of 1911 and had recently caused one of those minor campus sensations when he published an indictment of the Chapel System. This evening he absolutely glowed over the fact that some parents now considered him unfit to teach their sons. For Cornford, sharing the same platform with Bernard Shaw represented a communion of the saints of the heretical movement. Therefore G.B.S. had to fidget through a lengthy introduction in which Cornford characterized him among other things as a "protagonist of the heretical movement" and "one who never scrupled to tell his audience exactly what his opinions might be on religious questions" which was hardly news even in 1911 for anyone who had ever heard the name Shaw. Thunderous applause greeted these mild observations, but Shaw cut the applause off with upraised hands as he literally bounded to platform center, ready for action.

G.B.S. began by dismissing the flattery almost curtly. The subject of "The Future of Religion" was a serious one and he asked for serious attention. Actually, the Heretics were not the people who needed this lecture. The people who needed it were the orthodox people. As G.B.S. put it: "A Heretic is like a man with a mechanical genius who begins tinkering with a bicycle or a motor car and makes it something different from what the manufacturer has made it. . . . The Heretic is a sort of person who, no matter what religion is supplied at the shop—by which I mean the nearest church —he will tinker at it until he makes it what he thinks it should be . . . we need not bother about him. . . . What we want to trouble about is the great mass of people who take religion as they find it—as they get it at the shop."[7]

Shaw here would make the first of the quick little strides he substituted for pauses to indicate that he was ready to enter the next phase of his speech[8]—in this case to outline for the orthodox people what was needed in the way of a new God, a God who made sense in the context of the twentieth century. To build a workable religious system one simply had to find a God one could understand and G.B.S. insisted: "It is no use falling back on the old evasion and saying that God is beyond our comprehension. . . . Better atheist than agnostic: an agnostic is only an atheist without the courage of his opinions. The actual, practical use we can make of our God is that we can establish laws and morality which we suppose to be the will of God, and if we do not understand God's purpose we cannot do anything of the kind."

Shaw was warming to his task as was always said to be obvious in one of his speeches when he began to take strides forward, as well as sideways on the platform. G.B.S. was willing to admit, he told his audience speculatively, that there were certain special problems involved in the notion of Englishmen making a new and workable God, much less in accepting Shaw's own original doctrine of a God of the Life-Force, a doctrine which he nevertheless wished to propound later in this very speech. The trouble about an Englishman understanding about a practical God was that an Englishman never heard the word God outside of his place of worship. Ah, suddenly remembered Shaw, probably snapping his fingers and affecting delight, the courts of law were an exception at that. One did hear the name of God when some poor devil of a witness was going through the preliminary form of committing perjury or when the judge put on the black cap to sentence an unhappy wretch to death. As the audience of Heretics began to chuckle, G.B.S. grew even more arch and concluded mock-sadly that, of course, in Parliament one never heard the name of God at all.

Then, too, he averred, it might be late in the day to begin to talk about Englishmen making a God because of a strange paradox inherent in the religions of Europe. Historically Europeans had been less than creative in arriving at a fundamental God but had always been content to accept a sort of Oriental or Middle-Eastern religion as the nucleus of their own. These foreign religions contained legends and biblical stories that had long outlived their usefulness. Naturally, the day for even pretending to accept such nonsense was also long past. The man naive enough to believe the story of the Gadarene swine would believe anything, and in the name of humanity something had to be done to help him.

Next Shaw slipped into a rather long ironical passage in which he railed at the popes and kings and governments who had tended to profit from the inherited religions of the East. The audience of Heretics was responding beautifully to his irony and he was the very incarnation of the comical

"G.B.S.," but Shaw himself apparently grew restive. He was anxious to sweep away the religions of the past with a final loud blast so that he might go on to present his own new and shining doctrine of the Life-Force. Therefore, assuming the mantle of the democrat, G.B.S. now professed to see historical developments that gave him a gleam of hope after all that English soil might have become fallow enough to receive the seed of his own advanced and prophetic religion. On such climactic occasions G.B.S. was prone to pump his elbows back and forth in an odd gesture that tended to make his military erectness less pronounced as when now he declaimed:

> In democracy we are trying to get human nature up to a point at which idolatry no longer appeals to us. We see that in revolutions, like the French Revolution, democracy went first to the cathedrals and knocked off the heads of the idols of stone. Nothing happened. No crash of thunder stunned the universe, the veil of the temple remained intact. Then the people went to the palaces and cut off the heads of the idols of flesh and blood. Still nothing happened. . . .
> We are gradually getting more and more rid of our idols, and in the future we shall have to put before the people religions that are practical systems, which on the whole we can perceive work out in practice, instead of resulting in flagrant contradictions as they do at the present. . . . Darwin . . . made us familiar with that particular form of evolution known as natural selection. That idea was seized upon with a feeling of relief— relief that the old idea of God was banished from the world.

The Heretics applauded when the name of Darwin was mentioned. The statement that the old idea of God had been banished from the world by a Darwin would cause consternation and rage in contemporary newspapers, but for this congenial audience of Heretics, Shaw's magnetic tones had rendered the assertion a perfectly normal one. In fact, even

G.B.S. was probably somewhat worried that the undergraduates would be all too willing to accept Darwin's natural selection and survival of the fittest as a proper substitute for religion. Darwinism had never even begun to satisfy Shaw. Natural selection meant a universe that depended upon accident rather than on purpose and design. As G.B.S. told the Heretics:

> . . . But if there is no purpose or design in the universe the sooner we all cut our throats the better, for it is not much of a place to live in.
>
> Most of the natural selection men of the nineteenth century were very brilliant, but they were cowards. We want to get back to men with some belief in the purpose of the universe, with determination to identify themselves with it and with the courage that comes from that.

Shaw paused. He had dispensed with all the systems with which he wished to dispense. Obviously, the time had come for the grand affirmation of his own system—a modern religion of the Life-Force for the twentieth century. Shaw was equal to a crescendo effort for the occasion. At such times even the propulsion of his elbows tended to grow more intense. The Shavian head was thrown back, his eyes seemed to pierce through and beyond his auditors, and his voice deepened into a more pronounced Irish accent as his tone became prophetic. Yet for all the Shavian sincerity, for all his conviction that projecting his religious credo was the most important task, this section of the speech proved to have the least appeal to the audience of Heretics, to the newspapers, and to all commentators except Chesterton. Later Vincent Brome would characterize this portion of the speech as "distinguished by a mystic concentration only intelligible to the very deeply initiate," and that seems a fair appraisal of the reaction to it. Certainly the questions asked of Shaw immediately after the speech indicated that the Heretics themselves had not the faintest understanding of or interest in what Shaw had been talking about at this juncture. The newspapers would find headlines in all the negative statements G.B.S. had made but would leave his positive statements on his own religion relatively untouched. Only Chesterton would once again find himself in the classic position on G.B.S., the position that he had so precisely put before everyone in his book: "I am the only person who understands him and I do not agree with him." Only Chesterton seemed to realize G.B.S.'s high seriousness in this matter of his religion, and although the orthodox G.K.C. disagreed with the Shavian religion chapter and verse, he was also the only critic to respond to it seriously and to answer its propositions with dignity as well as humor.

To make it possible to understand what Shaw conceived to be "The Future of Religion" and to understand G.K.C.'s *Reply* it seems appropriate here to list as briefly as possible the major points in the Shavian religion as G.B.S. explained them in his own words on that long ago night in 1911:

> . . . As for my own position, I am, and always have been a mystic. I believe that the universe is being driven by a force that we might call the life-force. I see it as performing the miracle of creation, that it has got into the minds of men as what they call their will. . . .
>
> To attempt to represent this particular will or power as God—in the former meaning of the word—is now entirely hopeless; nobody can believe that. . . . Let me therefore ask you to think of God . . . as something not possessing hands and brains such as ours, and therefore having to use ours, as having brought us into existence in order to use us, and not being able to work in any other way. . . . If we accept that conception we can see the limitations of our God and can even pity him. In this way you can imagine that something—the life-force —through trial and error, beginning in a very blind and feeble way at first, first laboriously achieving motion,

making a little bit of slime to move, and then going on through the whole story of evolution, building up and up until at last man was reached. . . .

We are all experiments in the direction of making God. . . . We are not very successful attempts at God so far, but I believe that if we can drive into the heads of men the full consciousness of moral responsibility that comes to men with the knowledge that there never will be a God unless we make one . . . we can work towards that ideal until we get to be supermen, and then a world of organisms who have achieved and realized God. . . . Make the best religion you can . . . and then, when the different races of the earth have worked out their own conceptions of religion, let those religions all meet and criticize each other, and end, perhaps, in only one religion, and an inconceivably better religion than we now have any conception of. [Applause]

Shaw's speech was to inspire a number of questions as well as applause from the audience of Heretics. Recovering quickly from the solemn effort of propounding his religion, G.B.S. answered most of the questions on the facetious level. To one undergraduate who wondered what Shaw's religion offered as external expression to replace the liturgical pleasures of churchgoing, G.B.S. replied that the symphonies of Beethoven and the plays of Bernard Shaw would do nicely. To another who inquired whether or not "the Religion of the Future" contained the promise of a life after death, G.B.S. replied promptly that it did not. Further, he, Shaw, was ordinarily willing to disclaim any personal desire for future immortality but since Mrs. Shaw was present and his views might disturb her, he preferred to use restrained language on the subject this evening.

The response that was to prove most inflammatory with the newspapers, however, concerned Shaw's conception of Christ. G.B.S. told a young Heretic quite frankly, that he considered Christ one of the attempts, and ultimately, one of the failures, in realizing God. In fact, the man who considered Christ the highest attempt at realizing God was not worth working with. All of the newspapers were to print that assertion. Fewer were to report that G.B.S. had also begged not to be misunderstood, that while he thought Christianity had been to a great extent a failure, he did not mean to depreciate the great work upon which Christ had helped, the work of at least attempting to realize God, the work of pressing on to the good, to the superman.

The meeting concluded on a mild and pleasantly conventional note. First, the Heretics accorded G.B.S. a hearty vote of thanks. Then G.B.S. rose to accept the invitation of the Heretics to become a pledged honorary member of their Society. Later, the Society of Heretics was to reprint a reconstructed shorthand account of the Shavian address, dated July 11, 1911. All in all, the response of the Heretics to Shaw had been calm and mature.

Outside the Cambridge lecture halls the response to "The Future of Religion" was not comparably serene. The *Daily Express* for May 30, 1911, ran the account of Shaw's speech under the headline "Christ a Failure," and when G.B.S. refused by telegraph to retract what he had said, *The Academy* for June 3, 1911, exploded under the head "A Detestable Outrage":

> The question whether Mr. Shaw has beliefs or none may interest an egregious egotist . . . our protest is against the dissemination of poisonous theories amongst young persons . . . but we do not observe that the lecturer was kicked out of the window, or that he was thrown into the Cam . . . unless public attention is called to the vile and blasphemous ravings . . . it is unnecessary to resort to coarse profanity to teach the doctrines of materialism. . . . Socialism must now stand forth naked and unashamed as resting for its sanction upon flagrant infidelity.

A month later the protests had hardly diminished but the rhetoric had grown more orotund and studiously balanced as is evident in this sampling of the *Fortnightly Review,* July 1911:

> When a crowd of undergraduates assembles to hear Mr. Shaw proclaim that no man who looks upon Christ as the highest ideal is worth working with; when an utterance which is, at least, an unwarrantable assault upon some of the loftiest and noblest spirits of our time and something of an insult to the most sacred of our dead, is made within the time-honoured walls of Cambridge University for the edification doubtless of some of the sons of those who simply and straightforwardly hold a high faith . . . it is surely time for a chivalrous revolt against this conventional unconventionality.[9]

Actually the Society of Heretics was exhilarated by the sensation Shaw's speech was causing and hit upon the delightful notion of inviting G. K. Chesterton to reply to it in an address that should be titled "Orthodoxy." Then the public could not miss how scrupulously fair the Heretics wished to be about according the "other side" a hearing. G.K.C. was equally delighted to accept the invitation and to contest Shaw's premises on religion with which he disagreed totally. At the same time G.K.C. was aware, as the Heretics were not, that serious problems would confront him in attempting to refute the brilliant Bernard Shaw. For example, although he had been engaged to dispute G.B.S., Chesterton knew that he would have to begin his address by defending Shaw against the absolute nonsense that had been written about "The Future of Religion" in English newspapers and reviews. Therefore G.K.C. was in danger of confusing his audience of young Heretics from the outset. He might indeed emerge from the Guildhall looking much more the heretic than Shaw and just as much a storm center. Yet such confusion must be risked because G.K.C. had really been revolted by what had been written about G.B.S. and he had no alternative but to hit the Shavian critics hard. Before G.K.C.'s speech was a minute old, he would be saying:

> I must mention what appears to me the very absurd fuss made about the lecture delivered to the Heretics by Mr. Shaw. I have seen passages in "The Academy" that appear to me not merely written by an idiot [Laughter] but by an idiot who had no belief in the Christian religion. . . . How could Mr. Shaw blaspheme by saying that Christ or the Christian religion had failed in England when the remark is obviously true. I happen to believe myself that Christianity is the true religion but I do not believe for one moment any more than Mr. Shaw that England is a Christian country; rather we are separated from Christianity. For instance English economists and philanthropists have dared to propose a heathen idea like slavery, for certainly the idea of forbidding strikes and the complete enrolment of workers under one State system is slavery. [Applause] It is the first mistake of my side, the Orthodox side, to assume that the Commonwealth is a Christian country . . . the majority of the governing classes believe in no religion. I have known many editors and newspaper proprietors but I have yet to meet one who believed in religion. . . . Therefore I say that it is absolutely absurd in the modern world to try to interfere with a man like Mr. Shaw by calling him blasphemous. It is as absurd to attack Mr. Shaw for blasphemy as it would have been for St. Peter and St. John to attack Tiberius for blasphemy. Mr. Shaw is living in a comparatively Pagan world. He is something of a Pagan himself and like many other Pagans, he is a very fine man.[10]

Had Chesterton not uttered a word beyond this sensible defense of Shaw, his trip to the Guildhall would have been justified. Unfortunately, one often does have to justify G.K.C. and to forgive him much when he is being evaluated on his performance as a public speaker. Brilliant as his defense of Shaw might be in the passage cited above, its meandering prose already gives a clear indication of a damaging fact about G.K.C.—that he seemed constitutionally incapable of preparing a polished main speech in the manner of a G.B.S. In fact, at a first hearing of both one would think that only an enemy would choose to compare the faltering and stumbling G.K.C. with the firm and precise G.B.S.

In every facet of the speaking art G.K.C. seemed the very antithesis of the accomplished G.B.S. First, Shaw took pains to be as punctual as he was orderly about delivering public speeches and his consideration made a good first impression on an audience. Chesterton almost invariably arrived late and in some disarray. He was even late on this November evening in 1911 although he must have realized that the opportunity to make a *Reply* to a major address by Bernard Shaw constituted a significant step forward in his speaking career. G.K.C. had arrived at the Guildhall a full fifteen minutes late and wheezing apologies to Chairman Cornford and to between eight and nine hundred Heretics who had long since filled almost every seat. In this case G.K.C. was fortunate because the Heretics proved to be in an amenable mood and accorded him an ovation. Then, as he was able to do so often, G.K.C. proceeded to justify the ovation by talking wisely and wittily for two hours, taking one hour to deliver his main speech and one hour to answer questions. G.K.C. might arrive late, but on the credit side he worked hard when he did arrive and he seldom spoke more than five minutes before every listener knew that this was a man whose speech contained unusually deep values and insights. Nevertheless (although his admirers may still try to gloss over the fact), audiences sometimes deeply resented his tardiness, especially those audiences which had paid to hear him lecture. G.K.C. was by no means universally successful in overcoming this initial resentment while for Shaw initial resentment for this particular cause never existed.

Nor was Shaw prone to the personal idiosyncrasies which marred G.K.C.'s effectiveness as a public speaker. Even G.K.C.'s weight, something he was apparently helpless to do anything about, entered the picture. At age 37 in 1911 he already weighed 280 pounds[11] and appeared clumsy and obese although he did move with an odd and unexpected grace. Unfortunately, G.K.C. was very self-conscious about his size and made altogether too many jokes about it in his speeches. Another distracting element was the inadequate use G.K.C. made of notes that he had scribbled on sheets of paper that were multicolored and of varying sizes. Often a sheet would flutter to the floor unheeded during a speaking performance. When he held the notes too close to his leonine head and peered at them his voice became so muffled that an audience had to strain to hear what he was saying. He was more effective when he dispensed with his notes entirely, which he always did long before an evening of speech making was over. Then the audience could be distracted only by the crooked pince-nez which kept slipping from his nose to his massive chest. Finally, G.K.C. did not even sound particularly like a public speaker, partly because he never troubled to learn the art of public speaking and partly because his voice, while pleasant, had never come close to deepening in proportion to his size.

One might legitimately wonder, as many have, how the owner of such inadequate physical equipment ever emerged as incontestably one of the best debaters of his age. After listing some of these same faults in G.K.C. as a lecturer, Maisie Ward wrote: "Until G.K.C. turned up, G.B.S. had the world of controversy to himself. But as soon as G.K. stepped into the ring he had to watch his step in a new way, and make the most of his ring-craft. G.K. could always get through the old man's guard; and that made it especially exciting when they met."[12]

Miss Ward gives a simple reason for the apparent contradiction between G.K.C.'s faults as a speaker and his accomplishments. She insists on a sharp distinction between Chesterton, the lecturer, and Chesterton, the debater. She maintains that G.K.C. was a poor lecturer, "not only faltering in his manner but only too obviously unprepared." In debate, however, she claims it was just the opposite. G.K.C. was a great debater. To Miss Ward, "the contrast between G.K. lumbering through a lecture and G.K. carrying a fight to his opponent in a debate was complete."

Like many black and white explanations, Miss Ward's is something of an oversimplification. Actually, despite the rambling prose he employed, G.K.C. could be an extremely good lecturer. Intense self-awareness and self-knowledge enabled him to compensate for most of his handicaps. To begin with, G.K.C.'s approach to a major speech was much more methodical than his critics imagined. The fact that he did not write his speeches out beforehand could be sufficiently deceptive to lead an overconfident opponent to quick doom. Actually his preparation for the *Reply* to "The Future of Religion" had been quite complete. He had begun by making a serious study of Shaw's speech in the pamphlet issued by the Heretics in July of 1911. Then he had made himself familiar with every line that G.B.S. had ever published about religion as well as with the criticism published about G.B.S. on the subject. Writing the speech out was the single preparation that G.K.C. had failed to make beforehand. Even this was a calculated maneuver. G.K.C. was capable of composing a polished speech. Chesterton, the writer, could always give good competition to Shaw, the writer. Their styles were so remarkably similar that each could play with imitating the other and both enjoyed doing so.

On the other hand, Chesterton, the speaker, could not give good competition to Shaw, the speaker. G.K.C. could not deliver ringing lines without sounding ridiculous. Soaring words and thoughts demand a resonant voice to carry them, and G.K.C. did not possess a resonant voice. Most important, G.K.C. was completely aware of his limitations. The absent-minded body housed a practical mind. (Shaw had insisted in "Chesterbelloc" that if one were ever to understand Chesterton he would have to remember that G.K.C. was half French by descent and almost totally French in his rationalistic and realistic approach to solving a problem.) Over the years, G.K.C. had discovered that when he did not write out his speeches beforehand, his remarks took on a quality of spontaneity and unexpectedness in which an audience seemed to delight. Further, as G.K.C. rambled along in a pleasant conversational tone, his solid background of preparation would come into play, and he had ready to hand homely analogies and whatever range of analysis his audience of the evening seemed to require. These qualities, added to G.K.C.'s gift for repartee and sense of humor, offset his handicaps as a speaker and made him a dangerous opponent even when he was contesting a lecturer of the caliber of G.B.S.

On the evening of Friday, November 17, F. M. Cornford was again in the chair as he had been for Shaw's speech. His introduction was elaborate, and throughout it the applauding Heretics continued to demonstrate all good will to G.K.C. as they had to G.B.S. Nevertheless Chesterton was prepared to go all out in an attack on their champion Shaw if indeed it were fair to classify G.B.S. as a champion of heretics. For as G.K.C. once confided to G.B.S. at a lunch, he was always a bit mystified at the adulation of heretics for Shaw. Plainly Shaw was more on the side of the angels than he was on the side of heretics. Always G.B.S. had done his Shavian best to make it clear that he was not concerned with the destruction of religion but with the affirmation of a new religion, his own, a highly unorthodox religion, a religion objectionable to a Chesterton, but a religion nevertheless. Even in "The Future of Religion" G.B.S. had affirmed a need for a God of mystic origin and for a universe with a firm purpose behind it in terms that, it seemed to G.K.C., no self-respecting Heretic could accept but which this same audience of Heretics had not only accepted but had applauded throughout.

Certainly G.K.C. would not take issue with these affirmations of Shaw, his sincere efforts in the direction of a God and a purposeful universe. All that G.K.C. disagreed with were the Shavian findings in his search for God. All that Chesterton objected to and would attack was the particular God of the Life-Force which Shaw was trying to palm off on the public. G.K.C. sincerely believed that this business about "we are all experiments in the direction of making God" was complete nonsense. He had no qualms about confusing the Heretics or offending G.B.S. by blasting these aspects of Shaw's religion.

Moreover, G.K.C. knew that in this instance he was not quibbling by countering casual remarks by G.B.S. on a casual subject. In "The Future of Religion" Shaw had been talking about a religion which mattered passionately to him. In 1911 Chesterton was one of the few men in England who realized precisely how much this religion meant to G.B.S. Actually it is now known that in "The Future of Religion" G.B.S. had given a peak performance on a subject he had been trying to organize and to master since his first attempt at it in the speech "The Religion of the British Empire" delivered at the City Temple in London in 1906. As Warren Smith said of that and succeeding speeches: "He was then fifty, and his religious ideas were fully formed. His religion was a long time in developing but it proved durable."[13]

When Shaw delivered "The Future of Religion" address in 1911 he was fifty-five years old and had been in his prime as a speaker on religion for five years. G.B.S. had presented to the Heretics in long but carefully jointed sentences a full historical treatment of religion. He had capped his account by unveiling an intriguing modern alternative, his own religion of the Life-Force. Such a Shaw would be proud to stand on the record of his speech. Such a Shaw, G.K.C. realized, would welcome this challenge by an upstart apostle of the old orthodoxy like Chesterton.

If G.K.C. had intended to clash head on with Shaw's philosophy of religion, the stage and mood were being set perfectly on this November evening by the challenging introduction accorded to him by F. M. Cornford, Fellow of Trinity, and perennial chairman of the Society of Heretics. Cornford had been colorful enough during Shaw's visit, but he had since achieved a new status concerning the issue at hand and was now determined to strike a few sparks of his own even before G.K.C. could get up to speak. It seems that Cornford, emboldened and inspired by the frankness of Shaw's "Future of Religion," had contrived to make a formal address on the subject himself in the intervening months. In his own speech before the Heretics, Cornford had castigated Christianity and its role at Cambridge University. The press had given Cornford's speech good coverage, and only the week before G.K.C.'s arrival the Society of Heretics had decided to print Cornford's remarks verbatim. Chairman Cornford had been delighted and now found room to make a few coy and arch references to his own new-found "notoriety" as, warmly enough, he introduced G.K.C. in this vein:

> I suppose Mr. Chesterton is the only living man who has ever written two books, one entitled "Orthodoxy" and the other "Heretics." I have never read "Orthodoxy" having, I suppose, been repelled by the title [Laughter] but during the last twenty-four hours I have managed to read "Heretics". . . . I do not accept or

share Mr. Chesterton's religious views, though as a wit and a man of letters I have long admired him [Applause]. Finally it is my duty to carry out the direction of Mr. Ogden, the President, by explaining that the Heretics are not responsible for Mr. Chesterton's opinions any more than they were for those of Mr. Shaw.[14]

If G.K.C. thought it odd that Chairman Cornford had deserted the traditional role of neutrality to state his own point of view which incidentally coincided with that of G.K.C.'s opponent Shaw, he gave no sign. If he thought it humorous that the Heretics found it necessary to put on the record that the orthodox G.K.C. speaking on the subject "Orthodoxy" was not expressing their views, there is no record that he smiled. Instead G.K.C. rose amiably to an ovation and went right to work. Assuming, and maintaining throughout, the conversational and confiding tone that was most effective for him, G.K.C. immediately captured and held the attention of the Heretics, dissolving them into laughter many times along the way.

G.K.C. began by explaining that his late arrival was due to the fact that he had come here in a Cambridge cab and had constantly encouraged the horse and driver to go slower and slower so that he might see the beauties of the town and also make up what he was going to say. At that, he was not quite sure whether or not to apologize for being late. After all, the Heretics had sort of tricked him into this speech against his friend Mr. Shaw. The Heretics had sent him a beautiful invitation to speak, specifying that he might really speak on any subject he chose, but then, rather slyly and pointedly, had enclosed in the invitation the pamphlet recording Mr. Shaw's speech on "The Future of Religion." The inevitable had happened just as the Heretics might have surmised that it would. He had found himself reading and studying the pamphlet not only because he had enormous personal respect and affection for Mr. Shaw but also because everything Mr. Shaw ever wrote was worth reading. At the same time, of course, he had found himself, as always, disagreeing entirely with all the wonderful "stuff" Mr. Shaw had written. Then in a moment of weakness he had given in. He had sat down and written to the Heretics just what they probably intended him to write. He wrote that he would be happy to address the Heretics and, of course, the only thing worth speaking about and the only thing he wanted to do was to contradict the fearful nonsense Mr. Shaw had spoken to them. Now here he was in the Guildhall stuck for something to say.

Actually, as G.K.C. chatted on, it became evident that he knew exactly what he was going to say. Even the casual-sounding exordium had rendered his audience not only attentive but also benevolent and docile in the Ciceronian tradition of the exordium's function. By implying that the Heretics had tricked him on to the platform, he had added a nice touch—he had flattered the audience into thinking it was a step ahead of its speaker.

Once the audience was his, G.K.C. settled down to the business of the evening. First, he dismissed the outlandish and slanderous press reports on Shaw's speech and religious position, as recorded earlier in this chapter. Then he proceeded to make a point by point attack on Shaw's speech but only in areas where he thought G.B.S. might be validly attacked. All the vehemence and shrillness of the vicious newspaper assaults on G.B.S. were missing in G.K.C.'s approach. Instead, keeping his tones conversational but firm, he disputed Shaw's logic, most often by means of homely and humorous analogies. For example, he pounced upon an analogy G.B.S. had used himself in defining what the Heretics were. Shaw seemed to believe, chuckled G.K.C., that Heretics found a machine such as a motor car and by brilliant tinkering changed it into something different. Good enough. G.K.C. himself did not mind if people changed all the old sewing machines that seemed to be strewn all over London into bicycles. That sort of conversion was legitimate—but: "I strongly object to a person riding a bicycle, turning it into a sewing machine and then trying to ride the sewing machine." In a quiet sentence G.K.C. talked through laughter and applause to point out that his own analogy represented Shaw's confused view of religion. After all, this whole business of Shaw's "We must come together and make a God" was nonsense in the true meaning of the word "nonsense"—it was devoid of logic; it literally made no sense. Again, Chesterton resorted to analogy to make his point irresistibly clear:

> Supposing Bernard Shaw had said to you: "Here are five poor children. They haven't got a mother; let them come together and manufacture a mother." I think this audience will agree there is a certain well known slip in the logic of that observation. [Laughter] . . . Of course, if any friendly family desires to deceive itself deeply enough in the interests of survival by calling its eldest child mother or God, I don't object. I simply doubt whether it will advance human thought very much. [Laughter] It is perfectly obvious that when men talked about God, they had meant a large number of ideas, but they certainly had not meant something produced by the people who were thinking about it. . . . What is the good of talking about a God who is not made yet but is struggling to exist. The thing is again a contradiction in terms. The moment a thing has begun to struggle it has begun to exist. There is no such thing as *trying to exist*. But apart from the mere logical lapse here, I want to point out that there would be absolutely no value in that kind of God anyway because first we want something *fixed* in a God by which we can regulate ourselves. All that Mr. Shaw said was that instead of being a jolly atheist he preferred to think there was some deity struggling at the bottom of the universe

somewhere who would also turn up somewhere and say Mr. Shaw was right in what he said. [Laughter]

Chesterton was blunt enough in dismissing Shaw's religion of the Life-Force. He reserved his most trenchant blast, however, for G.B.S.'s version of the historical relationship between democracy and the decline of organized religion. G.B.S. had declared that there was now hope for enlightened religions like his own to make their way because democracy had destroyed the old idols of stone and the old idols of flesh and blood in such events as the French Revolution. The statement had been too strong for G.K.C. to accept with any degree of equanimity. Actually, G.K.C.'s own teeth had probably begun to grate at the very notion of Socialist Shaw setting himself up as "a democrat to the teeth" for the purposes of this lecture. In *George Bernard Shaw* he had already argued that G.B.S. had not the faintest notion of what democracy meant. Now, before the audience of Heretics, G.K.C. was able to reiterate and add to the same point in the much plainer terminology he employed on the platform:

> Mr. Shaw says that democracy means the destruction of idols. Why should it? Of course, it is characteristic of Mr. Shaw that he knows no more what democracy means than I know Chinese. Democracy means a very simple thing, really. It means that if we are snowed up in this lecture room which, for the purposes of debate, I hope we may be, everyone in this audience of Heretics should have a say in what should be done. If, for example, the members of the audience decide to raid the platform and kill me, or put a Gatling gun on the table, or try any other of the forms of human government, it would be done by a majority decision. In a word, democracy need have nothing to do with the destruction of idols.

Now Chesterton took the dangerous plunge that had caused many an unwitting Shavian opponent to be skewered.

He questioned a Shaw fact. G.K.C. had himself warned debaters to beware of the apparent hyperbole G.B.S. employed because actually Shaw was scrupulously careful about his facts and research and delighted to pounce on anyone who questioned them. Unsuspecting vivisectionists, astronomers, historians, and literateurs often learned this to their sorrow. Nevertheless, Chesterton was sufficiently confident in his own facts and sufficiently wrought up over Shaw's attempt to twist the French Revolution into a declaration of independence from organized religions to declare bluntly:

> Mr. Shaw said that democracy meant the destruction of idols and he stated that when the French revolutionists marched they first cut off the heads of the saints in the cathedrals. They certainly did not! This is an error in fact. This is historically inaccurate. That was not the sequence at all. What the revolutionaries did first was to declare as principles a number of very rigid metaphysical dogmas which I happen to think are true. Apparently the members of the aristocracy did not. There followed a very natural quarrel between the aristocrats and the revolutionaries who believed that they had been sold out to the enemy. Only then did the revolutionaries cut off the heads of the idols and they did not then first cut off the heads of the idols of stone; they cut off the heads of the idols of flesh and blood. Mr. Shaw, as usual, is talking his own inspired brand of erratic nonsense.

Now Chesterton called a halt to attacking Mr. Shaw. It seemed appropriate to conclude by stating his own religious position. Then the Shavians in the audience would have more opportunity to defend their champion by attacking G.K.C. in the question period to follow the lecture. G.K.C. made clear that he was not merely inviting questions. He was inviting attack. The audience literally cheered G.K.C.'s bold challenge. (This was the sort of approach that is unfailingly popular with university audiences.) Chesterton quickly put on the record that his own religious position was close to Rome's. He realized it would surprise absolutely no one to hear that he really did prefer Christianity in its unadulterated form. He expected that some would be startled, however, and more would think he was joking when he admitted publicly what had attracted him to Rome. Christian theology had originally won G.K.C.'s respect when he found it to be based on Reason and Freedom. A quick burst of laughter actually did greet G.K.C.'s statement. To many of the Heretics, Reason was missing from the approach of Christian theology to the realities of the twentieth century. To more of the Heretics a history of excommunications, censorship, and Inquisition had rendered the Roman Catholic Church the very antithesis of Freedom.

Yet Chesterton talked through the laughter to insist that Reason and Freedom were the twin cornerstones of the Roman Catholic Church and of all Christianity. Any system that had endured for nineteen hundred years among brilliant and sincere men, as well as among scoundrels, must have had some basis in Reason. G.K.C. had had no difficulty in accepting that to begin with and his studies had confirmed to his satisfaction that Christianity was a reasonable religion. Chesterton admitted that it was much more difficult to establish, and almost impossible to prove, the second half of his proposition—that Freedom was also basic to Christianity and its God. Nevertheless, he was convinced himself that God had not only intended to set humanity free but had intended that his creatures should then become creators in their turn and be responsible for the worlds they created. Man himself had abused his own freedom by perpetrating all sorts of evils in its name. Even then God had not intervened because of the risk of removing the gift of freedom he had bestowed. As G.K.C. put it:

> God is standing aside from the evils in the world today, not as Mr. Shaw suggests because he is unable to interfere with things bigger than Himself, but as a great and magnanimous King who says, "I have sent my son into the world and he must do his best." It seems to me once God had set humanity free, he could not keep it bound at the same time. It seems to me that setting humanity free was so inspiring a conception that one might forgive God or any other being all the risks and troubles that such freedom might involve. Which do you, my hearers, prefer, the absurd baby God of Shaw's, kicking in the cradle, or the great King who prefers his knights to be chivalrous and free? . . . [Applause]—End Address.[15]

When Mr. Cornford rose to moderate the question and answer session, he requested the audience "to lash Mr. Chesterton into fury as he had begged." If the audience attempted "to lash Mr. Chesterton into fury," it failed. The audience did succeed in something much better. It elicited from Mr. Chesterton what the *Cambridge Daily News* called "the most enjoyable part of the proceedings . . . he dealt with his many hecklers in a very prompt and ready manner, replying immediately and at considerable length to every query. . . . The result was an exhibition of dialectical skill such as is rarely seen at a public meeting."

Chesterton did seem to handle the thorniest questions with remarkable ease. If the slightest chink appeared in a question, the questioner was doomed. For example, one man wanted to know whether Reason and Freedom still lived in Christian Theology when the Catholic Church suppressed Pascal. That question would seem to call for a very defensive answer. Yet, by seizing on the name "Pascal," the solitary chink, G.K.C. turned his answer into an immediate triumph:

> Of course Reason and Freedom still lived in the Church when the Jesuits suppressed Pascal. Does my questioner or anyone else in the room know what Pascal and the Jesuits were arguing about? I will tell you and I think you will then agree that the Church had to do something about the situation. Pascal had taken it upon himself to deny that Reason could lead a man to God. Pascal had denied that Liberty or Freedom entered into the question at all. Pascal said that God deliberately damned some people. The Jesuits said no, that God really wanted every man to be good, to escape hell and to save his soul. Pascal refused to accept this. He insisted that God deliberately meant that some people should not have the grace to enable them to overcome their temptations. The Catholic Church shut Pascal up because Pascal denied Reason and Liberty. On which side are my hearers now that you have heard the real issue? On which side is the whole civilized world? Pascal happened to be a much greater man than the men who suppressed him but in this case he was wrong and they were right.

The Chesterton wit was also in evidence, especially when he wanted to cut off a discussion that threatened to grow too theoretical and tedious. Witness the sudden end to this passage-at-arms:

> THE QUESTIONER: Mr. Chesterton, you should never say you "know" unless you have scientific proof. I say "I have an intuition."
>
> MR. CHESTERTON: You know you exist?
>
> THE QUESTIONER: No, I would be very careful to avoid the word "know." I should say "I have an intuition I exist."
>
> MR. CHESTERTON: So much the worse for you. I am fairly certain that you do exist. I am absolutely certain

that I exist. It is incorrect to say a man cannot be certain of anything unless he has scientific proof right at hand.

THE QUESTIONER: My dear Mr. Chesterton, this is merely a matter of definition. I use the word in a different sense. I say it is perfectly true that I have an intuition that I exist.

MR. CHESTERTON: Cherish it. [Laughter and applause.]

A most impressive quality in G.K.C. as a debater was his maintenance of certain limits beyond which he refused to exchange his sincerity for refuge in the clever or funny answer. A case in point occurred as the hour grew late and the meeting at the Guildhall neared its close. Just after Chesterton had insisted that reason was essential to religious belief, a man asked him the legitimate but embarrassing question: "How do you reconcile that position with a belief in miracles?" Without resort to any form of verbal side-stepping, G.K.C. answered flatly: "I have always believed in miracles even before I believed in Christianity. I have never been able to see why spirit should not alter matter, and I have never been able to see the philosophic objection to miracles."

Outright statements like this led *The Gownsman,* a publication which favored the position of Shaw and the Heretics, to comment almost sadly on G.K.C.:

> It was a rare pleasure to watch the agility with which he pounced upon the gist of motive of a question, his scrupulous fairness, his exacerbating aplomb. Deplore as we may the dissipation of endowments of such breadth and profundity in acceptance of the Miraculous and the palliation of Papal Oppression we must be grateful indeed to a speaker who can occasionally introduce Humour into the Divine . . . we have an intuition that few representatives of the Creeds can be so sympathetic to the aims and ideal of the heresy as this Apostle of Toleration and Goodwill—and we hope he will allow us to "cherish it."[16]

The Gownsman went on to declare G.K.C.'s Cambridge meeting a "personal triumph." Indeed the press was unanimous in its general approval of Chesterton's performance. One paper did express surprise that such an avowed Heretic as Cornford had been allowed to preside in the Chair. Nevertheless, it had been Mr. Cornford who rose to "propose a hearty vote of thanks to Mr. Chesterton," when G.K.C. concluded his remarks. When the audience responded to the proposal with prolonged applause and cheering, it had been Mr. Cornford also who ended the evening graciously by saying, "Cambridge has to thank Mr. Chesterton for a unique and most enjoyable evening."

The press was also quick to pair the Shaw-Chesterton speeches as a unit, and both men came off favorably as a result. *The Christian Commonwealth* for November 29, 1911, noted, "Mr. Chesterton, like Mr. Shaw, was at his best—the very incarnation of G.K.C." *The Cambridge Review* for November 23, 1911, had perhaps best summarized the general reaction: "We congratulated the Society on the occasion of Mr. Shaw's visit, and we do so again: Shaw-Chesterton—one name only can render the matter complete."

When Shaw learned in London the favorable impression young Chesterton had made in attacking the Shavian ramparts, he was delighted. He resolved to debate G.K.C. He made an appointment to have lunch with him to arrange the details. This was the major result of the first Shaw-Chesterton "speaking contest." It led to the debates. Perhaps the only flaw in the speaking contest had been that the two men had not shared the platform on the same evening to debate such a permanently interesting topic as "The Future of Religion." Unquestionably, G.B.S. would have enjoyed the opportunity to retort to Chesterton's version of the bicycles and sewing machine analogy. Nothing less than a Shavian explosion would have greeted G.K.C. when he dared to question

Shaw's factual account of the French Revolution. When shortly after his speech he met G.B.S. for the luncheon, G.K.C. fully expected to be harangued for his thrusts at "The Future of Religion." Instead Shaw disarmed the younger man completely by making only one oblique reference to his address and that in a bantering tone: "I'm a likable old rascal you know—but you really must stop poisoning my mind with all these heresies about God. Otherwise I shall really have to go for you." And Chesterton, amazed at this gentle rejoinder to his full scale attack, could only respond: "It's your intellectual magnanimity which destroys me. If only you were a nasty fellow who lost his temper."[17]

Chesterton was learning with dramatic speed that G.B.S. was one of the last men in the world to waste time nursing rancor over old issues. Hardly had the ink dried on the favorable notices for G.K.C.'s speech than G.B.S. had become much less concerned about "The Future of Religion" than he was about the future of Shaw-Chesterton. G.B.S. had discovered a new and brilliant opponent. In 1911 new and brilliant opponents were rare commodities for G.B.S. He was anxious to test the young man immediately in a debate. He did not care a straw what the subject of debate would be. Now Chesterton was to learn also that once G.B.S. had set his purpose, he was not a man to let the details of arrangement bog him down. G.K.C. had delivered his "Reply" to Shaw on November 17, 1911. Thirteen days later, by November 30, 1911, Shaw had managed to place the mammoth G.K.C. on the stage of the Memorial Hall, London, and there the first actual, in-person debate between them took place.

five

DEBATES—FORMAL AND INFORMAL

Once the grand design of the first debate had been formed, G.B.S. and G.K.C. were more than happy to allow the contest itself to be conducted under the auspices of the Fabian Society since both were anxious to be relieved of the petty details of arrangement. The move proved unfortunate. A solemn committee of Fabians took their administrative role much too seriously and tried to impose a series of strictures on the debaters that, had G.B.S.–G.K.C. heeded them, could have spoiled the debate altogether. For example, G.B.S. and G.K.C. insisted that the orthodox Hilaire Belloc be Chairman of the debate. Reluctantly, the committee accepted the gruff Belloc for the post but did not permit him a single one of the interruptions for which he was famous. Belloc's sudden intrusions into a debate were the very spice on which G.B.S. and G.K.C. were counting to set the whole tone for a free swinging contest. G.B.S. had confided to G.K.C. by letter: "We both want Belloc to let himself go (I simply thirst for the blood of his Servile State—I'll servile him); and nobody wants to tie you down to matter previously introduced when you make your final reply. We should all three be allowed to talk all over the shop—possibly never reaching the Socialism department—and Belloc would not trouble himself about the rules of public meeting and debate even if there were any reason to suppose that he is acquainted with them."[1]

The spirit of what the men intended shines from that letter. Yet the record shows a muzzled Belloc and a G.B.S. and a G.K.C. limited carefully to speeches of 30, 15, and 10 minutes each. Chesterton always did chafe under Fabian shackles. G.K.C., a Fabian Socialist up to the time of the Boer War, had finally quit the Society in disgust because, as he claimed, he had been unable to make progress in the face of all those "webbed feet," a phrase, incidentally, which constitutes as succinct a putdown of Beatrice and Sidney Webb as can be found in print.

But not even the solemn Webbs could make the days of 1911 other than gay and sparkling for rank and file Fabians and for their friendly challengers as well. Nineteen hundred and eleven was the year in which Belloc and Chesterton rode into the Savoy Hotel on donkeys and demanded food, drink, and shelter for themselves and for their beasts. Shaw preferred bicycles to donkeys as a means of locomotion. In 1911 he was in the habit of cycling to Land's End, laughing and shouting greetings to bystanders all the way. Belloc liked to hike, too. In the first decade of this new century he had once walked all the way to Rome and immortalized his foot journey in *The Path To Rome* (1902), a joyous little book which has easily outlived his controversial tracts. Nor was the era demanding on those it loved. In 1911 a Shaw could draw guffaws by introducing G.K.C. as "a fellow of infinite vest." Even this outrageous pun was subtle compared to some of the broad histrionics in which the pair indulged. There was the night, for instance, when G.B.S. arrived first for a debate with the extremely popular G.K.C. On this night Shaw was foiled in his attempt to play out his self-assigned role of mock villain in the debates when the audience accorded him a standing and heart-warming ovation. G.B.S. leaped to his feet and said earnestly: "I am sorry, but I am not Mr. Chesterton."[22]

One night a chuckling G.K.C. became so engrossed in debating G.B.S. that he was completely unaware that he was keeping his audience on tenterhooks while his gold-chased chair creaked dangerously under his massive weight. Nor did G.K.C. ever become aware. He scarcely seemed to notice, as without interrupting a single sentence of his discourse, he shifted to a sturdier chair when the gold one finally toppled and splintered.[3]

Naturally, not even the most solemn Fabian committee could quell all that exuberance. G.B.S. and G.K.C. let plenty of it brim over on Thursday evening, November 30, the night of the first debate. Belloc at least tried to be dutiful and to follow the rules. As he introduced the first speaker, G.B.S., he pointed out that the committee had decided to limit the debate to the topics included in its assigned title "The Democrat, The Socialist, and The Gentleman." The ebullient Shaw refused to comply. He punctured the committee's stricture immediately by proceeding to make the assigned topic a verbal plaything. Then he set up for definition several alternatives to the announced topic of the evening. He did it all quickly in brisk, pungent language: "I assert that a Democrat who is not also a Socialist, is no gentleman. I say it in the most insulting personal sense of the term. I have to define the three terms, and their alternatives—the alternative to a gentleman which is a cad, the alternative to a Socialist for which I don't know the exact name; and the alternative to a Democrat which is an idolator."[4]

Next G.B.S. proceeded to present definitions of everything in sight, including brilliant definitions of Democracy and Socialism which still read like model textbook definitions of the terms. G.K.C., awaiting his turn to speak, recognized the brilliance of Shaw's display. Yet he was to prove his mettle as an opponent for G.B.S. by refusing to be awed. Rather, taking his cue from G.B.S.'s witty opening, he responded in kind and the fun was on:

> I approach this question with all the more diffidence and difficulty because of the extraordinarily brilliant and interesting address Mr. Shaw has delivered upon a totally different subject. The subject we are supposed to be discussing is an algebraical formula consisting of three unknown quantities—Democrat, Gentleman, and Socialist. I don't know whether I am a gentleman, I am sure that I am a Democrat and that Mr. Shaw is not a Democrat. . . . I don't know what is the social rank of a person like myself who presumes to be a gentleman and not a Socialist compared with the social rank of the gentleman who is a Socialist and not a Democrat, like Mr. Shaw.

Once G.K.C. had treated the audience to his own caliber of verbal by-play, he continued to emulate Shaw. He contributed definitions of Democracy and Socialism just different enough from those of G.B.S. and just brilliant enough to provide excellent guidelines of dispute for the evening. Both men were displaying the rare ability to make an audience chuckle and think at the same time. Nor can it be claimed that the feat was unexpected. Memorial Hall had filled early for the debate, so obviously the audience knew it was in for a unique treat. In this case fulfillment must have exceeded anticipation, because G.B.S. and G.K.C. never again debated before a house that was not overflowing as well as filled. Many were to remember this first debate as significant. Years later, Mr. Harry Craven, a lifelong Fabian, stated that the best speeches he had ever heard delivered in his entire life were "during a debate between G.B.S. and G.K.C. on 'a man who is not a socialist is no gentleman.'"[5]

Still, one no longer consults the G.B.S.–G.K.C. of 1911 for new insights on Socialism or Democracy. For another half century the terms have been defined and redefined according to changing political and social situations. One is even struck by how much more sophisticated the opinions of G.B.S. and G.K.C. themselves had become by 1927 in the last debate, "Do We Agree?" On the first night in 1911, G.B.S. and G.K.C. had been content to define terms, size each other up as debaters, and to enjoy themselves. Neither was attempting to erect monuments of intellectual advance in the fields of Socialism and Democracy.

Nevertheless, the debate is well worth rereading today for its brilliant style. Any student of debate can observe with profit the marvelous thrust and parry technique which necessity had forced G.B.S. and G.K.C. to develop in this very first debate. The men had discovered before the contest was an hour old that they were extraordinarily well matched in the ordinary procedures of debate. Therefore, it became necessary for each to spar warily until the one discovered what he conceived to be a fatal chink or flaw in the argument of the other. Then the very essence of the conflict became to hammer away at the chink until it opened into a wide gap. Victory in a G.B.S.–G.K.C. debate was often to hinge upon so narrow a margin as this. The two quickly agreed that almost any device from ridicule to scorn could be employed legitimately to gain the advantage. As a result reading a Shaw-Chesterton debate can be particularly profitable if one focuses on the areas in which the one utilized every technique of the debating art to gain the edge over the other.

For example, one can observe Shaw employing the "chink" or "flaw" motif masterfully in that debate on Christianity where he forces Chesterton at last to admit publicly that he believed in the most improbable sounding miracle of the periodically congealing blood of St. Januarius. In this first debate one should observe G.K.C. at work as, quite early in the proceedings, he discovers a similar opportunity to ridicule G.B.S.'s general thesis by exaggerating a single aspect of it.

The setting was this: The men had come to grips over the meaning of political equality. To G.K.C., the Democrat, equality meant equal opportunity, especially equal opportunity to own private property. To G.B.S., the Socialist, equality implied the collective ownership of everything, including property, by the State. Above all, G.B.S. insisted, equality meant that every man, woman, and child should possess absolute cash equality. When Shaw emphasized "cash equality" for every human being, G.K.C. went on the alert. Perhaps G.B.S. was providing him the "chink" he sought. If so, he was prepared to pounce. When his turn to speak came, G.K.C. leaned over the small raised platform, erected especially for the debate, and said in properly incredulous tones: "Mr. Shaw said Socialism means the absolutely equal payment to all human beings, without respect to class, sex or age. Does he mean that a new-born babe shall be at once in receipt, I cannot say enjoyment, of the income which would be right and proper to a grown, working human being? [Mr. Shaw: "Yes."] Well, it is barely possible a community might solemnly vote incomes of £500 a year to new-born infants but the alternative is much more probable, that wages would be cut down to the level of those of the babe."

On the equal income for babes issue G.K.C. had trapped Shaw in an apparent *reductio ad absurdum*. G.B.S. would have to frame arguments to put his principle of equal income for all into better perspective. In the meantime, however, G.K.C. was following good debating procedure by plunging ahead into new areas. The idea was to make all the gains he could before Shaw had a chance to retaliate.

G.K.C. did have a major objective at this juncture in the debate. Up to now G.K.C. had tried without success to establish for the audience sharper distinctions between Democracy and Socialism than Shaw would allow. Particularly G.K.C. had tried to contrast the private ownership principle of the Democrats to the collective ownership principle of the Socialists. Shrewdly, Shaw had vitiated much of the force of G.K.C.'s arguments by employing the time honored refuge of debaters and diplomats, the art of compromise. Why should his friend G.K.C. be all that doctrinaire a Democrat? He, G.B.S., was not at all that doctrinaire a Socialist. G.B.S. professed that a little private ownership was perfectly all right with him. Why would G.K.C. not admit that such private ownership might be combined nicely with collective ownership of major industries by the government? Then everybody would be happy, including the audience. The effect of G.B.S.'s conciliatory approach had been to frustrate Chesterton. G.K.C., as a former Socialist, had not been trying for one moment to convince the audience that Socialism had no values at all! Rather, he had been trying earnestly to convince the audience that the values in Socialism and the values in Democracy were totally different values, not at all so closely related as G.B.S. had suggested. Now G.K.C. stopped trying to depend upon closely reasoned argument to top the clever G.B.S. Instead, he came much closer to making his point, as was often the case with him in debate, when he depended upon one of his extravagant but surprisingly effective analogies:

> Supposing we all had wooden legs and were living together in a hospital, and there was a rule that we should take the wooden legs every night into the cloakroom and get a ticket for them. We should avoid a great many definite evils; one man could not steal another's wooden leg, or pawn his wooden leg, or make a corner in wooden legs. But if you want a society in which all men govern themselves, you have not advanced a single step by collecting and redistributing all the wooden legs. All you have done is to ensure yourself against certain kinds of evil which have nothing to do with democracy. You may think this is a monstrous and fantastic example.

I and a large number of people think that depriving an ordinary man of the direct and absolute sense of personal property is exactly like cutting off his leg and giving him a wooden one.

Then Chesterton went on to declare how profoundly the ordinary workingman did believe in the right to own private property. When G.K.C. talked about private property, he talked about the concept closest to his heart. An average Democrat could never emulate G.K.C.'s passion for the subject. In the end G.K.C. would even have to find a new name —Distributism—to distinguish his philosophy on the distribution of property from that of the ordinary Democrat. In the first debate G.K.C. came within an eyelash of describing fully this Distributism, as yet unnamed in 1911 but already identifiable in embryo as the principle of private property and peasant proprietorship. For convenience the philosophy will be referred to from here on as Distributism although it was not known to the public by that title at the time. Distributism would always remain G.K.C.'s solution to what he conceived to be the twin evils of Socialism and Capitalism. In the cause of Distributism, G.K.C. was even willing to let his rhetoric flow emotionally on occasion. One recalls that most often G.K.C. held his rhetoric in check because of his voice, which he once referred to himself as "the mouse that came forth from the mountain."[6] Yet in the first debate G.K.C.'s conclusion on private ownership and private property was quite emotional:

The poor have only one kind of property left. Years and years of enlightened Protestant progress have taken away from them any other kind. The poor still *do* manage to possess their own bodies. And for the Capitalists, who are not above using Socialist arguments to maintain that even this freedom of body could be detrimental to the community, could lead to an inefficient work staff and an insufficient food supply production, the poor have an answer. The poor answer as Naboth answered to that great ancient Socialist king, Ahab, who was also strongly opposed to peasant proprietorship . . . "The Lord forbid that I should give the inheritance of my father unto thee."

Shaw was not impressed. The principle of private property was not sacred to him. Perhaps, too, G.B.S. was somewhat annoyed with G.K.C. for exploiting the "equal income for babies" issue. To an outsider it might seem that G.K.C. had taken slight advantage of knowledge of Shaw gained through personal friendship. As G.K.C. must have known, most of G.B.S.'s colleagues would have shied away from public admission of belief in the concept that babies deserved an equal share of a state's income. Yet Chesterton had been able to proceed with confidence in his facetious and damaging references because he had learned that G.B.S. was of the rare breed who would never deny or make lame excuses for what he believed merely to score a debating point. Actually, G.B.S. was not so squeamish as to be annoyed because G.K.C. had used personal knowledge of him so effectively. Both men considered as grist for the mill of debate whatever one knew about the other. What probably did worry Shaw was the effect of G.K.C.'s thrust upon the audience. In scoring one debating point Chesterton might well have opened to ridicule the whole Shavian case for Collectivism. Perhaps Collectivism was not sacred to Shaw but it was of prime importance to him. G.B.S. decided to win back his audience by meeting the "equal income for babies" issue head on:

Mr. Chesterton says that I have defined nothing, and cannot, for the life of him, seem to make out what I am driving at. Well I see he made out clearly enough the "baby income" part of my definition of Socialism. Mr. Chesterton thinks fantastic my modest proposal that a baby should come into its dividend of the nation's wealth. Yet right now in this country, there are several babies who at the moment of birth came into £40,000 or £50,000 per year. . . . Mr. Chesterton also said that if the Socialists held command that wages would be cut down to the level of the baby. There is no objection to that if you give the baby the proper wage. I am not only in favor of the old-age pension but also of the life pension and of the baby pension.

Shaw's reply had been clever, although it does not follow logically that because some baby aristocrats inherit too much money, all babies are entitled to an equal share of the nation's income. Yet emotionally an audience melted and was much more receptive to the most magnanimous goals of Socialism when it was made dramatically aware of the inequity of the huge sums of money that baby aristocrats in reality did receive. Scarcely anything could have better reflected Shaw's experience on the podium than this adroit bid to draw the audience back into his camp.

Now G.B.S. was free to come to grips with G.K.C.'s exalted sense of property. Here G.B.S. was not to be completely successful. He had expected that G.K.C. would react sharply the instant he sought to alter the conditions for private ownership which Chesterton had deemed sacred. Instead G.K.C. perplexed G.B.S. by appearing bored and indifferent when Shaw launched an intensely serious attack on the status quo. This turn of events precipitated the following rather sharp exchange:

Coming to the objection that cutting off a man's absolute and direct sense of property is a calamity, I don't see where Mr. Chesterton and I are that far apart. . . . I, too, am willing to propose a certain distribution of property so that everybody shall have some. The only difference is that I say, for practical purposes it must be measured by equal income. [Mr. Chesterton, interrupting: "No!"] All right, I shall put it this way. I say that the State should distribute money, which gives a man

command of the things he likes, in equal proportions—
what do you say? [Mr. Chesterton: "I don't mind."]
That is trifling with the question; you must mind! I wish
I could persuade Mr. Chesterton that I really am a serious man dealing with a serious question.

Then Shaw inveighed against such industrial evils and inequities as he thought his friend Chesterton should oppose more
vigorously. Point by point he demonstrated how Socialism
could rectify such evils and inequities.

Now it was G.K.C.'s turn to grow vehement. Shaw had
finally nettled him. G.B.S. had implied clearly that G.K.C.
was indifferent to the Shavian attempt to change the status
quo. In reality G.K.C. respected G.B.S.'s aims. Mutual
desire to help the poor in society was one of the strongest
bonds of their friendship. G.K.C. had been indifferent to
Shaw's litany of attack against industrial evils in England for
a different reason than G.B.S. had suspected. When he rose
to speak, G.K.C. made immediately clear why he had been
bored: "I cannot understand why so dextrous and brilliant
a debater as Mr. Shaw should have wasted so much time in
attacking the present system of industrial England. Who
except a devil from hell ever defended it? I detest it as much as
he does." Nor did G.K.C. agree that G.B.S.'s Socialism could
rectify the evils of Capitalism. Still a bit roused but the better
debater for it, he explained why he disagreed with G.B.S.

> Mr. Shaw must get clear that I object to his solution
> of Socialism not because it will be a violent change but
> because it will be . . . devilishly *like* Capitalism. . . .
> I do not care whether the man who deals out the money
> is called Lord So and So, and is the employer and head
> of the great soap works, or whether he is still called Lord
> So and So (as he probably will be) and called the Social
> Administrator in the name of the State for the same soap
> works. . . .
> The proposition I put in the place of the one Mr.

Shaw ought to have maintained is, that if you want self-government apart from good government, you must have a generally distributed property. You must create the largest possible number of owners.

Chesterton was moving smoothly now. He had neatly equated Socialism to Capitalism. He had quite skillfully drawn his own Distributism back into the debate. He was scoring debating points. He even contrived, as a last sally, a random reference to that figure of fun and contention, the wage-earning baby: "I pause for a moment on the baby. Mr. Shaw said that the baby would receive wages. Does Mr. Shaw mean that every infant is to be detached from the labor and responsibility of parents? If so, the whole human race will violently disagree."

The last sally failed. It was simply impossible to write G.B.S. off as a home wrecker. G.B.S. was able to dispose in two or three sentences of the notion that he might favor an unnatural intervention between baby and parent: "Mr. Chesterton says a babe should be dependent upon its mother. As if I had been suggesting that it should not be! He must know that, as now, the income must be given to its mother and guardians, and spent for it."

G.B.S. had handled this point easily. Still, G.K.C. was working well. He had matched G.B.S. definition for definition. He had continued to exploit the "baby" chink. He had argued a plausible case for Distributism against Socialism. He had already proved that he would make an excellent foil for G.B.S. in any debate. More menacing to G.B.S. in the competitive sense, G.K.C. seemed to be operating from a position of growing strength as the debate wore on. If one were adjudging a victor, he could classify G.B.S.'s position at this point as "hard-pressed."

Still, the redoubtable Shaw had retained his calm and confidence throughout and he had had good reason to retain his poise. For G.B.S., too, had discovered a chink and, as it developed, a rather vital one in the Chestertonian argument. Shrewdly he had attacked Chesterton just often enough on the point to keep the elusive G.K.C. within possible range of a dramatic Shavian debating coup. Oddly, G.K.C.'s vulnerable point had turned out to be a facet of his Distributism, the very area of the debate to which he was committed most, both intellectually and emotionally. At first, G.K.C.'s Distributism had intrigued G.B.S. Involving as it did the distribution of property among the greatest number of owners, the idea had sounded attractive even to Socialist Shaw. G.B.S. had been quite sincere when he argued that, as far as he could make out, G.K.C.'s position did not seem to differ fundamentally from his own. Then, as G.K.C. rolled on, a little doubt began to assail G.B.S. How did G.K.C. propose to distribute the property? By what practical means? Quite early in the debate G.B.S. had asked: "Since Mr. Chesterton does mean apparently that everybody is to have their share, what is the share to be? Are you to have more or less than I? Is any man to have more than another? If so, why? Is any man to have less than another? If so, why?"

When G.K.C. avoided answering this spate of questions, Shaw grew genuinely puzzled. As the debate wore on, he began to repeat the same questions more and more insistently. G.K.C. continued to ignore any question involving the practical administration of Distributism. Then G.B.S. became frankly skeptical. Only one reason could explain Chesterton's silence. G.K.C. had not answered because he had no answer! The history of Distributism has since proved G.B.S. correct in his reasoning. In the normal probing of debate G.B.S. had been skilled and fortunate enough to put to G.K.C. the one question about Distributism he was not as yet prepared to answer in 1911. Once G.B.S. had absorbed this fact, he never let his audience forget it.

At the same time G.B.S. had no illusions. He was not so naive as to conclude that in uncovering a technical flaw in Distributism he had uncovered so colorful and comic a flaw as G.K.C. had been exploiting all evening. One does not easily match an "equal income for babies" issue for humorous or crowd-pleasing effects. Chesterton was having most of the fun. Nevertheless, Shaw, the debater, knew that he had discovered the more significant argument in the scale of the debate's values. An objective witness would now have to concede that Shaw had done much to buttress his thesis that the practical value of Socialism outweighed the practical value of Distributism. When Shaw rose for summation, he was willing to place the Socialism-Distributism comparison in the climactic position for the audience's final consideration. At the very end he would still be insisting that G.K.C. explain how Distributists intended to distribute: "Mr. Chesterton wants a distribution of property, and the only difference between him and the Socialist is that the Socialist says there shall be equal distribution. If you agree with me that it should be in equal proportions, you are a Socialist. If you do not agree, in heaven's name, I ask you for the last time, will you tell me in what proportion you want it distributed?"

Again G.K.C. ignored G.B.S.'s exhortation. He did not yield the faintest clue as to how a Distributist proposed to distribute. Instead he delivered a marvelously vague peroration extolling the panacea-like virtues of Distributism, i.e., of private property and peasant proprietorship. At one point he got so far afield as to suggest that a form of Distributism was working out quite well in certain remote parts of Asia!

Here and there in the first debate, each man had been guilty of a glaring lapse. G.K.C. must have lost debating points when he failed to demonstrate how Distributism could function equitably. G.B.S. showed discomfiture, if not embarrassment, when G.K.C. continued to reduce his argument of equal income for babies to absurdity. Still, perspective must not be lost. Overall, the audience had been witness to an excellent debate. Moreover, few partisans of G.B.S. or G.K.C. could quibble seriously today if the long ago debate, reread and evaluated, were adjudged a draw.

Most important, G.B.S. and G.K.C. had also set the pattern for future debates in this first duel. As the audience had expected, the two men had proved well-matched in the standard procedures of debate. However, Shaw had emerged quite clearly as the better of the two at presenting a thesis, at sustaining an argument, and at sheer attack for the sake of attack. G.K.C. had demonstrated that his forte was counterattack. Chesterton had a superior gift for precise, point by point counterargument and for total counterattack on a general thesis. Difficult as it is to generalize on such an extraordinary pair, this pattern of G.B.S. on attack and G.K.C. on counterattack may be said to have remained fairly constant throughout the debates. Almost invariably the persuasive Shaw, the man with the well-prepared and well-reasoned thesis, would make the best first impression on the audience. However, G.B.S. sometimes fell victim before the fact that it is much harder to sustain a thesis than to tear one down. As a result, the affable and more casual Chesterton, the man who nevertheless possessed and produced the precise counterarguments, most often seemed to grow stronger as the debate progressed. Most often, but not always! The very charm of this pair was that each could suddenly break out of any mold. Then all set criteria dissolved, usually into laughter—their own and that of the audience.

For Shaw a wry footnote existed to the first debate and to all the debates that involved the principle of G.K.C.'s Distributism. G.B.S. must have had to work hard to resist the temptation to exploit publicly the rich irony that pervaded the concept of G.K.C. as champion of the workman, champion of peasant proprietorship, and champion of rural life. First, it was impossible for G.B.S. to listen to Chesterton speak in tones that bordered on the Cockney and to forget for an instant that this advocate of the precipices, crags, and fields was as confirmed a city dweller as Samuel Johnson. Shaw wrote that G.K.C. resembled Dickens' cockney, Sammy Weller, in everything except size and education. Like Sammy, G.K.C. had found his first romance not on moor and fen but in the London streets and in picking his way across Battersea Bridge in the midnight fog.

Second, G.B.S. could not help but notice that, physically, the clumsy and unwieldy giant with whom he debated was the absolute antithesis of the lean, hard, bronzed workman whom he idealized. G.K.C. would have been at a loss as to how to wield a pick or spade. He could not possibly have survived a month in the individualistic society he had envisioned.

Privately, G.B.S. loved to tax G.K.C. with the incongruity between his person and his position. Publicly, he never did. Shaw was all too aware that his friend Chesterton was making speeches not to improve his own lot but to improve the lot of the working man. G.K.C. might cut a ludicrous figure at times, but he was sincere when he hailed peasant proprietorship as an alternative to Shaw's collectivist principles. Both men possessed to an uncommon degree the ability to work for motives that transcended self-interest. Other intellectuals might profess desire to do the same on certain ceremonial occasions. The record proves that on a day-to-day basis G.B.S. and G.K.C. did devote a major share of their special talents to the service of mankind. When Bernard Shaw and Gilbert Chesterton debated, the only real victor was truth.

G.B.S. and G.K.C. continued to debate Religion, Socialism, and Distributism down through the years. Fortunately for the entertainment value to audiences, only their motives remained constant. The ideas of G.B.S., for example, were always in flux. G.K.C. was pressed to new ingenuities to counter them. The language, analogies, and sallies of the contestants seemed to grow increasingly pungent and entertaining as the years rolled on. The warriors spoke their last formal words on Socialism and Distributism in 1927 in "Do We Agree?" a debate Cecil Palmer published as a book the year after it was delivered. Yet to find the best verbal exchange between G.B.S. and G.K.C., that is, the best verbal exchange preserved in writing, one does not look into the record of any of the formal contests. One looks instead into the record of a spontaneous debate that took place on a night in 1923 when the disputants met entirely by chance at the home of a mutual friend in Chelsea. On that night the language of G.B.S. and G.K.C. was to coruscate and flame as never before or since. Religion was the catalyst. The two men lost their tempers in a sharp disagreement over religion. Before equanimity had been restored, Shaw and Chesterton had also flared up on Socialism, on Distributism, on Puritanism, on all the issues closest to their hearts. Flashes of Chestertonian and Shavian wit punctuated the battle, but the wit only served to veil thinly the intensity and gravity of the discourse.

Everything about the chance meeting of the combatants was fortuitous and calculated to reveal the pair at their uninhibited best. The most important fortuitous circumstance was the presence of Hesketh Pearson, future biographer of Shaw and friend of Chesterton, who published a verbatim report of the encounter in *The Adelphi* of London for September, 1923. Louis Biancolli, who made a study of remarkable conversations, was highly appreciative of Pearson's contribution. He considered Pearson's presence and the stenographic action he undertook a story in itself, one of the rare strokes of good fortune in the history of conversation.[7] Later Biancolli would insist that only from Pearson's own description could one understand properly the atmosphere of the debate including the light-hearted but very real esteem in which G.B.S. and G.K.C. were held in 1923. Reread today, Pearson's account appears wildly overdrawn, but his breathless prose does capture the flavor of the era when G.B.S. and G.K.C. rode their literary crests:

> I had for years longed to be present at a word-war between intellectual giants. And at last, most unexpectedly, my desire was gratified. It was at the house of a friend in Chelsea. Mr. Bernard Shaw had been there for at least an hour and was just on the point of leaving when Mr. G. K. Chesterton was announced. They instantly started a debate, as naturally as a cat and dog start a fight, and the rest of us grouped ourselves round them, as naturally as street loiterers surround the cat and dog. Consider my position. It was both fortunate and difficult. To begin with, my wildest dream had been realized. Here were, beyond comparison the two greatest word-jugglers of the century. One of them was a greater man than Socrates—yet I knew he had no Plato. The other was a greater wit than Johnson—yet I knew he had no Boswell. Could I, then, enjoy myself to the full and take no thought for the morrow? Did I not rather owe a duty to posterity, and was I not bound to preserve, at any rate, ten minutes of that feast of reason and that flow of soul which, but for me, would be lost to the world forever?[8]

Obviously, for the exuberant Pearson the clash between G.B.S. and G.K.C. contained more than passing significance. Even a Shavian or Chestertonian might wince a bit at the exalted company in which Pearson placed G.B.S. and G.K.C. as conversationalists. It is at least barely possible that Socrates and Johnson have as much staying power among the immortals of conversation as G.B.S. and G.K.C. Nevertheless Pearson was definitely on the side of the angels. For as Biancolli observed, if Pearson displayed the adulation of Boswell, he also displayed his thoroughness. Any adherent of G.B.S.– G.K.C. must be grateful for Pearson's next act: "I only had about half a minute to make a decision. Well, I was not conscious of making a decision at all. I simply know that my hand went to my pocket book—posterity no doubt guiding it there in spite of myself—and before Mr. Shaw had got the first sentence off his tongue my pencil was busy."

The debate itself was a rousing one and came close to justifying Pearson's exuberance. Several factors besides the natural skill of the debaters contributed to its pith and excellence. For example, G.B.S. was not at all inclined to be his usual temperate self when he met G.K.C. on the evening of the debate. Rather he was in a contentious if not snappish mood. Not long before the meeting G.K.C. had confounded many of Shaw's claims and predictions for him by having himself received as a practicing member into the Roman Catholic Church. This was the fact which would lead to the loss of tempers. Shaw had been more than irked by the news. For the moment he had refused to accept as fact that G.K.C. intended to bow humbly before the authority of Rome. Even the physical notion of G.K.C. kneeling in a confessional, to do penance and to receive absolution, was distasteful to Shaw. His temporary pique led him to make some cutting remarks which not only upset the affable G.K.C. but turned the debate into a sometimes fierce verbal melèe. At one point there was even a mild exchange over *George Bernard Shaw*. Since G.K.C.'s old book had been published a full fourteen years previously, its mention provided a strong indication that this night in 1923 was to serve as a clearing house for all grievances old and new.

The setting was perfect for an uninhibited exchange. Since the men were arguing in a private home and not on a public platform, they could afford to be, and were, astonishingly frank. The drawing room audience was quite literate so that the men were free to conduct the contest on a high literary plane. It was often said that G.K.C. liked to talk more than he liked to drink and that G.B.S. substituted the delights of talk for the delights of the meat and drink he forswore. That night each poured forth words as though no other listener existed. Each, apparently, was completely unaware that Pearson was inditing every word.

No time was wasted on preliminaries. Shaw opened verbal fire on Chesterton at sight. G.B.S.'s greeting was also quite unsubtle, and cold print alone does not reveal the reason for G.K.C.'s apparently airy reaction to it:

> SHAW: Have you any adequate excuse to make us for not being drunk?
>
> CHESTERTON: I am desperately drunk. There is only one form of drunkenness I acknowledge—the drunkenness of sobriety. As a consequence of not having tasted a drop of wine or ale today, I am suffering from *delirium tremens.*
>
> SHAW: In that case you will please tell us why you are sober.
>
> CHESTERTON: That, I fear, is quite impossible. I can explain nothing when I am sober. Sobriety clouds the mind, drink clears it. I would explain anything, at any length, under the calming, clarifying influence of drink. If only you would take my advice, your own style, to say nothing of your mind, would improve beyond imagination. At present your writing is too parenthetical; you wander, lost in a maze of speculation, in a pool of prudery. Compare with your straggling sentences my crisp phrases. I dip my nib in the pot of Bacchus.

G.K.C.'s parry of G.B.S.'s initial thrust had seemed lighthearted. In reality the parry constituted something of an act of restraint. According to William Irvine,[9] G.K.C. had been quite disturbed by the rather rude tone and implications of Shaw's sudden inquiry into the state of his sobriety. Only after an awkward pause had G.K.C. smiled and decided to answer G.B.S. on the facetious level. He had had no quarrel with G.B.S.; he hoped G.B.S. had no serious quarrel with him. Perhaps his facetious approach would bring Shaw back to his gracious self. Chesterton's device worked only partly. Tonight G.B.S. was not even in the mood to accept as genuine G.K.C.'s avowed admiration for wine. Still, about the wine, G.B.S. did make one brief attempt to rise to G.K.C.'s bait and to engage in typical G.B.S.–G.K.C. badinage: "SHAW: I don't believe it for a moment. Your pretended love of wine is a snare and a delusion. It is skillfully paraded and exploited by yourself in order to catch all the brainless bairns who look to romance to lead them back into the Garden of Eden."

Then, quite suddenly, Shaw dropped his bantering tone and turned somewhat sour. Apparently, G.B.S. was struggling with his better nature and losing the struggle. Now he proceeded to explain the bewildered Chesterton to himself in harsh terms. The gratuitous explanation included a singularly unflattering resumé of G.K.C.'s career in Socialism, in Distributism, and in Religion. Actually, G.B.S.'s explanation was more an attack than an explanation. The attack started mildly but grew progressively bitter and personal. Worst of all, G.B.S. seemed to question at every turn the sincerity of G.K.C.'s motives or, at the least, to assign to him motives of expedience. This was not typical Shaw-Chesterton. This was talk that could blast a debate wide open:

> SHAW: Of course, you are superlatively clever; no one denies that. And the cleverest thing you ever did in your life was to hang out the signboard of medievalism. You suddenly realized with a shock that there was no room for a second Shaw among the modern intellectuals. Were you daunted? Not you! You in-

stantly proclaimed to the whole world that you had examined Socialism and found it wanting. Actually you had examined nothing except the state of the book-market, a very cursory glance at which revealed to you that the camp of reaction lacked a brain to give its ideals—or want of them—expression. . . So what did you do? You talked about Guilds, about Peasant Proprietorship, for all the world as if Henry V were occupying the throne of Edward VII, and by carefully evading every knotty point in the Socialist case and riding roughshod over the unanswerable, annihilating logic of the Fabians which cropped up at every turn, you managed to rally all the wild, romantic idiots in the country round your banner. Then . . . you professed yourself a High Churchman and a deep drinker. Your slogan became: Back to the land, back to the priest, back to the bottle. . . . Whether you ever seriously believed in it, whether you have ever seriously believed in anything, I am quite incapable of deciding, since you don't really know what you believe or disbelieve yourself.

Although G.B.S. had not reached the crescendo of his speech, his attack had already grown quite sharp by the norms of standard Shaw-Chesterton. The vehemence of tone and language precluded the possibility that G.B.S. was play-acting. If the startled G.K.C. had been at all puzzled over the root cause of the Shavian pique, G.B.S. was not to leave him any longer in any doubt. Shaw proceeded to particularize Rome and Roman Catholic associations as the factors responsible for the fall from grace by his friend G.K.C. Even today the scorn that informed the Shavian attack is capable of leaping forth from a sampling of the prose:

But there dawned a day—a terrible day for you—when Hilaire Belloc came into your life. Then indeed you were lost forever. He made you dignify your monstrosities with the name of Faith. For you, at any rate, he turned your pranks into prayers, your somersaults into sacraments, your oddities into oblations. By degrees, under his influence, your fun turned to fury. Because the Roman Church says that the indiscriminate breeding of babies is the first duty of civilized man—meaning, of course, babies born for the Church of Rome—you turned and rent the Eugenists, whose sole crime is that they prefer healthy babies to diseased ones. You even suggested that Sir Francis Galton, a charming old gentleman of unblemished moral character, must have been a prurient blackguard whose loathsome lewdness was fitly camouflaged by the imposition of this obscene science upon the world. With viperish violence, and under the same influence, you then fell upon the Jews. Forgetting, with characteristic absence of mind that Jesus Christ was distinctly Hebraic, you implied that all the dark and dirty dealings in the world were directly traceable to the malign activities of that race. . . . And yet we all know perfectly well that you aren't half as bad as you paint yourself.

Shaw, obviously struggling to get a grip on himself, had finally introduced milder subject matter. He insisted, for example, that Chesterton did not drink the quantities of ale his public imagined, certainly in the Shavian view a salutary fact. Although happy to note G.B.S.'s attempt at conciliation, G.K.C. seized on Shaw's compliment to point out it was a compliment only a Puritan would pay. Then G.K.C. reminded G.B.S. facetiously that in the book *George Bernard Shaw* he had proved "up to the hilt" that Shaw was a Puritan and that G.B.S. had never been able to answer the charge. G.B.S. sounded almost his old self as he rejoined: "I have spent my life answering it both before and since the appearance of your book—which, by the way, might just as well have been entitled: *Gilbert Keith Chesterton by Himself.*"

No one was more relieved than G.K.C. when the dialogue returned, even temporarily, to normal channels. Odd as it may seem, G.K.C. had found it impossible to remain

angry with Shaw once he had discovered that the cause of
G.B.S.'s anger had been his own conversion to the Roman
Catholic Church. First of all, Chesterton had understood for
some time that his odyssey to personal religious certainty,
ending in Rome in 1922, had been incomprehensible to
many of his other friends as well as to Shaw. In fact, despite
signposts like *Heretics* (1905) and *Orthodoxy* (1908), some
of G.K.C.'s contemporaries actually regarded his conversion
to Roman Catholicism as a stunt. In his *Autobiography*
(1936) G.K.C. was to point out that at this stage his problem was frequently not to get people to agree with his beliefs, but to accept the fact that he believed them. Especially,
this must have been G.K.C.'s problem in the case of G.B.S.
For if G.K.C.'s casual contemporaries had cause to be
puzzled by his conversion, if even Belloc professed to be surprised by it, then Bernard Shaw had every right to be as-
tounded as well as embarrassed. G.B.S. had for years understood Chesterton better than any man alive in most areas
that involved intellectual and spiritual persuasion. G.B.S. had
been positive that the Roman Catholic Church was no place
for a man of G.K.C.'s temperament and intellect. He had
been so certain that G.K.C. was his own intellectual kinsman,
a member of his own spiritual family, that he sometimes considered it a personal affront when an observer expressed the
conviction that G.K.C. might wind up in the Roman camp.
As late as 1916, G.B.S. had written:

> Mr. West had also heard that I am "an avowed and utter
> Puritan"; and that Mr. Chesterton is "a Catholic Tory".
> . . . But both statements are overdone: they are the
> literary equivalents of burning down the house to roast
> the pig. I should roughly class John Knox among the
> famous fools of history, and Calvin among its most
> famous scoundrels; and the spectacle of Mr. Chesterton
> on his knees every Easter before a Creature of like pas-
> sions (in homeopathic dilution) with himself and much

less brains; confessing his sins and receiving absolution, is one which the world has not yet seen. . . . I suggest, therefore, that this use of Puritan and Catholic as abusive epithets, though exhilarating, is apt to mislead those who are not in the family.[10]

Shaw had had reason to speak with conviction about G.K.C. Still the fact that a man like Chesterton could be at the same time a rationalist, a Christian, and logically consistent to his own satisfaction, was one truth which was always to remain outside Shaw's vision. In the midst of the shock that had overwhelmed him when he first heard that G.K.C. had become a Roman Catholic, Shaw had written to his friend immediately:

> This is going too far. I am an Irishman and know how far the official Catholic Church can go. Your ideal Church does not exist and never can exist within the official organization in which Father Dempsey will always be efficient and Father Keegan[11] futile if not actually silenced; and I know that an official Catholic Chesterton is an impossibility. . . . I believe that you would not have become a professed official Catholic if you did not believe that you believe in Transubstantiation; but I find it quite impossible to believe that you believe in Transubstantiation any more than, say Dr. Saleeby does. You will have to go to Confession next Easter; and I find the spectacle—the box, your portly kneeling figure, the poor devil inside wishing you had become a Fire-worshipper, instead of coming there to shake his soul with a sense of his ridiculousness and yours—all incredible, monstrous, comic, though of course I can put a perfect literary complexion on it in a brace of shakes. . . .
>
> Now, however, I am becoming personal (how else can I be sincere?).[12]

Chesterton had accepted this letter in good stead. In the letter Shaw had expressed his anger at what he considered to be the foolishness of G.K.C.'s reception into the Church of Rome but nowhere in it had he impugned his friend's sincerity. If anything, G.B.S. and G.K.C. had always been rather prone to fight a mutual battle side by side to establish each other's sincerity before the world. Yet tonight in the Chelsea drawing room conditions were different. Tonight G.B.S. was making a travesty of G.K.C.'s sincerity in politics and in religion. Perhaps it was the face to face confrontation with G.K.C. that had exasperated G.B.S. Simple truth and verbal cleverness, as has been said, are not so soundly wed in a drawing room where one speaks in front of people as in the leisure of a study where one writes a letter.

Whatever Shaw's motives, his attack verging on tirade sparked an excellent debate. William Irvine exaggerated slightly when he wrote: "From this point quarter was neither asked nor given." Yet Irvine was precisely correct in that all the dialogue which followed was spirited and much of it brilliant. The only reason it could be said that Irvine exaggerated was the incontrovertible fact that G.K.C., the more positive of the two on this particular evening, did mellow as the evening progressed and made several efforts to conciliate Shaw, although G.B.S., caught up in a mood, never did quite shake off his irascibility. As a result, the recorded dialogue much better supports Irvine's other contention: "Chesterton seems to have been the more constructive and finished more strongly."[13]

For example, Chesterton seems to have made a genuine attempt to set the stage for Shaw to hear calmly the real reasons for his conversion to Rome and the real reasons that he had found solace in the Roman Catholic viewpoint. After the digression on Puritanism G.K.C. had said to Shaw challengingly: "The real case against you is not that you prefer Bunyan to Shakespeare or John Knox to Mary Stuart or Shelley to Byron or Ibsen to Pinero—but that you are constitutionally incapable of understanding the Catholic standpoint, which is, I need scarcely say, my own standpoint."

In response, G.B.S., still impatient, had merely ridiculed G.K.C.'s intellectual maunderings and religious questings, at one point likening him to a Don Quixote and Sancho Panza rolled into one. Shaw was still Shaw, however. He had phrased his condemnation of G.K.C.'s motifs so skillfully that he set up one of the better exchanges of the evening. G.B.S.'s Quixote-Panza image even provided G.K.C. an opening to get his religious viewpoint on the record at last. The pertinent part of the exchange ran like this:

SHAW: How in thunder can I understand a point of view that doesn't exist? Your standpoint is that there is no standpoint. . . . There is not a single principle in the universe that you have ever seriously attacked or seriously defended. . . . You fight . . . not in order to win . . . but for the mere pleasure of fighting. . . . You are just like Don Quixote; and though your lunacy on some occasions makes his seem pale by comparison, you yet contrive in some mysterious way to be your own Sancho Panza.

CHESTERTON: Exactly; and anybody but you could see that the combination of these two extremes forms the Catholic standpoint. . . . He (the Catholic) takes the whole world to his heart. He loves because it is human to love, hates because it is human to hate. . . . Life is contradictious and we are Life. We accept Life as a gift from God; we do not accept God as a gift from Life. You Puritans—

SHAW: I have already told you that I am not a Puritan!

CHESTERTON: You Puritans, I say, fashion God in your own image. You conceive the truth to lie in yourselves . . . you would recast it (the world) entirely to the highbrow's dream. . . . We Catholics . . . would not take it upon ourselves to say that this is altogether wrong, or that altogether right, because we think that

the wrong may be created by God for a purpose which
it would be presumptuous in us to divine. . . .

SHAW: I think I catch your drift. If a manure-heap close
to your front door were fouling the neighborhood, you
wouldn't remove it because God might have placed
it there in order to test your sense of smell.

CHESTERTON: I couldn't overlook the possibility that
my next-door neighbor might be a Socialist; in which
case the manure-heap would have its uses.

There was more, much more dialogue, of the same caliber.
Reread in *Great Conversations* amid Biancolli's exalted company of Socrates, Plato, *et al.,* the conversation, remarkably
literate, holds up and reads well. Overall, the exhibition ranks
easily as a superior example of spontaneous debate.

Studying the debate as literature, one can discover an
unusual fact about its close. At the very end, the debate
changed tone and lost completely its underlying note of high
seriousness. Suddenly Shaw and Chesterton seemed to run
out of steam and to become something less than themselves
and something more like refugees from a comedy of Oscar
Wilde. It is not obvious what caused the change, but the
debate ended on a complete note of *fin de siècle* effrontery
and witty insult. Perhaps the men had simply grown weary
of serious talk, or perhaps G.B.S. and G.K.C. were affected
by the drawing room gallery, laughing and applauding them
on. At any rate, the closing stretch of dialogue provided a
fascinating glimpse of how much, at times, even two towering
individuals like Shaw and Chesterton owed their personalities
and conversations to the nineties:

SHAW: You are evading the point.

CHESTERTON: Points are made to evade. Consider the
history of the rapier.

SHAW: There is no getting at you. You are as bad as Dr.
Johnson. When your pistol misses fire, which it usu-

ally does, you knock your opponent down with the butt end. Why will you never come to grips?

CHESTERTON: The art of argument lies in the ingenuity with which one can hide and seek simultaneously.

SHAW: But what becomes of your philosophy?

CHESTERTON: My philosophy is in the thrust, not the parry.

SHAW: I don't see that. You must be able to hold your own field while you are advancing on the enemy's territory.

CHESTERTON: Not necessarily. If my attack is strenuous enough, the enemy will require all his strength to hold his own fortifications.

SHAW: And if he succeeds in holding them?

CHESTERTON: Then I retire, bring up my reserves, and attack him again in a totally unexpected place.

SHAW: But if he attacks you while you are retiring?

CHESTERTON: I go to ground.

SHAW: I see. Heads you win, tails he loses, all the way.

CHESTERTON: Precisely.

SHAW: Thank you. I am wasting my time. Good evening. (*Rapid exit of Shaw.*)

One fact emerges from this last exchange. The display of froth and bubble might have been less rich than the display of wit and humor that G.B.S. and G.K.C. customarily produced. Yet it proved that Shaw and Chesterton along with their other conversational assets could improvise good Wildean dialogue—effortlessly—whenever they chose. The whole evening in Chelsea—including its footnote of a close—served notice that G.B.S. and G.K.C. were indeed a pair to remember.

In November of 1927, G.B.S. and G.K.C. delivered the last of the formal debates, "Do We Agree?" Shaw was seventy-one years of age, snowy of beard and mane, but hale. The huge Chesterton was not yet sixty but he was aging fast and had but nine years to live. Both were aware that the times and mood of the public had changed and that few really cared any more about their special versions of Socialism and Distributism. As a result, their performance as debaters in "Do We Agree?" might very well be compared to the aging Shakespeare's performance as a dramatist in his last major play, *The Tempest*. The bard was said to be a dramatist on holiday in *The Tempest*, obviously toying with and enjoying last experiments and analyses. G.B.S. and G.K.C. were debaters on holiday in "Do We Agree?" Only superficially did the debate seem the same as all the others. G.B.S. and G.K.C. were still debating Socialism-Distributism. Hilaire Belloc was still in the chair as he had been for the first debate in 1911. Yet all three were to give speeches which indicated clearly that they realized that the crowd in 1927 had turned out merely to be entertained by three old warriors of anachronistic mien and language. Belloc was a bit melancholy about the fact, but G.B.S. and G.K.C. were more than willing to humor the crowd and to enjoy the experience themselves. The two did not allow any more tense situations to develop in "Do We Agree?" than had Shakespeare in *The Tempest*. Like the play, the debate might be classified a good show, one in which two proven artists were enjoying a calm sunset of peace and reconciliation after whatever storms personal experience had brought to each. ˙

Actually neither had much to say that was startlingly new about Socialism or Distributism. G.B.S. was still insisting that Distributism was "plumb-centre" Socialism. G.K.C. was still politely insisting that it was not. As always, Shaw had done his homework and could quote (and did!) yesterday's newspaper to prove that the distribution of money and income in England was as grossly inequitable as ever. Chesterton was still capable of the homely but dazzling analogy. On this night he was to move the crowd to spontaneous applause when he twisted a fine analogy of Shaw's on the virtues of umbrellas as collectively owned property into a perfect proof that the umbrella was an even better example of the glorious right of the individual to own private property. Yet now in 1927 even G.K.C. had had to mute sadly his dream of peasant proprietorship in the face of the inevitable reality of encroaching industrialization and world urbanization.

The real value of "Do We Agree?" does not lie in its insights on Socialism and Distributism. The real value of "Do We Agree?" lies in the sophistication of argument and in the improvement of debating technique which the years had brought to G.B.S. and to G.K.C. Shaw's famous opening speech alone is worthy of the name of oral art. Another interesting aspect of "Do We Agree?" is that the mellowing G.B.S. and G.K.C. took time out in the body of the debate to make a fascinating comment or two on each other's literary techniques, something the socially impassioned pair would have been loath to do in their younger debating days when both were still out to reform the world.

Outside of the improvement in its literary form, "Do We Agree?" was fairly standard G.B.S.–G.K.C., but it became much more famous than any of the other debates. The fledgling B.B.C. broadcast the debate live, the newspapers reported it liberally, and in July of 1928, Cecil Palmer, a member of the Distributist League, published the debate as a book. Palmer took the pains to consult the debaters to verify the accuracy of his verbatim account, and he revised the speeches where the debaters reported he had not been accurate. In 1930 "Do We Agree?" entered the German language via the firm of R. Kayser, which published the debate in Bremen. As late as 1964 Haskell House of New York put out a particularly attractive edition bound in bright green and printed in a generously large and deep black-letter format. If ever a Shaw-Chesterton debate was "available" it is "Do We Agree?"

Nevertheless, a few loose ends about the contest remain to be bound up before an account of the debates can be said to be complete. Few have paid sufficient attention to reporting in detail the background of the debate, nor has anyone made more than sporadic allusion to its literary significance. Both elements are worth more than passing notice. Inexplicably, Cecil Palmer, who performed such salutary service in printing its speeches, did not even tell his readers where or when the debate took place, much less how it received such a provocative title (although Shaw himself did explain the odd nomenclature in one of his speeches).

The debate was held under the aegis of *G.K.'s Weekly,* the chaotic journal of the Distributist League, and this compounded the usual merry confusion that tended to surround a G.B.S.–G.K.C. venture. *G.K.'s Weekly* was itself in deep economic trouble, the result of hiring handsomely salaried new reporters while it was still trying to exist on its original capital and nothing more. W. R. Titterton, Assistant Editor, had been searching desperately for a scheme to raise money to help revive his ailing sheet. Ironically, he did not at first think of a debate between G.B.S. and G.K.C. although, by accident, he was to turn out to be the prime mover and cause of "Do We Agree?" Instead, Titterton, operating completely on his own, had gone to Bernard Shaw and asked him to write a couple of articles for *G.K.'s Weekly* to help stimulate sales. Had anyone else but Titterton asked Socialist Shaw to give aid and succor to the cause of the Distributism he despised, G.B.S. probably would have been shocked. But Shaw had recognized Titterton at once as the burly Sergeant-at-Arms at all Distributist League debates, an always friendly, sometimes brawling man for whom the adjectives "colorful" and "brassy" were too modest. Out of deference to their mutual friend Chesterton, G.B.S. did not want to be too hard on Titterton. At first, G.B.S. tried patiently to convince him that only a series of articles, carefully and expensively advertised, could help the circulation of *G.K.'s Weekly* and such a series he did not have the time to write. When this argument failed to convince Titterton, G.B.S. lost his patience and became blunt. "He replied," Titterton reported, "that he would certainly not write for *G.K.'s Weekly*. He hoped that the paper would die. Chesterton was wasting his time on it trying to establish a false antithesis between Distributism and Socialism, whereas in fact Distributism was plumb-centre Socialism. He thought that Chesterton would get into the new Jerusalem, but not on the back of half a dozen donkeys, not even on the back of as well-intentioned a donkey as myself."[14]

The ebullient Titterton took this rebuff as a triumph because it had given him an inspiration for a different means to help *G.K.'s Weekly* and the Distributist League. He went rushing to Chesterton with a new plan which in reality did not have much connection in logic with what G.B.S. had said:

> I told G.K.C. what Shaw had said and he roared with laughter. "Yes," he said, "Shaw's a fine chap." I looked at him in amazement. "Don't you see," I asked, "that we've got him?"
>
> "Have we?" said Chesterton. "Well, then what do we want to do with him?"
>
> I said, that here was Shaw maintaining that there was no difference between Distributism and Socialism, that, in fact, he and G.K.C. were in agreement. Let Chesterton take up the challenge; let Shaw be asked to debate with him on the subject "Do We Agree?" Shaw was bound to agree to *that*.
>
> "Yes," said Chesterton, "That's not a bad idea. I'll write to him."

That was how the debate "Do We Agree?" got its name and its format. Perhaps the oddest part of the whole story was that when G.B.S. received G.K.C.'s letter, he consented to the debate at once. Shaw did retain a qualm or two, though. When the contestants met to plan the debate, he said: "Look here, Chesterton, tell me frankly, is there really a Distributist League, or is it merely Titterton running in and out with a flag?"[15]

Shaw had consented to the debate because he seldom could refuse his friend G.K.C. a favor and because he was honest enough to admit that the idea of the debate, including its queer little question "Do We Agree?" appealed to him. Why not? Since 1911 Shaw had been genuinely convinced there was no need for Distributism because its principles were almost the same as those of his own Socialism which had the advantage of being a much better organized political system. Why should not G.B.S. expend one more evening of energy and skill to convince G.K.C. that they were in basic agreement? That way perhaps this Distributism nonsense could be dispensed with for once and all. Actually, G.K.C. was the whole unifying strength of the small Distributism movement, and to the Shaw of 1927, the brilliant G.K.C. had become the only Distributist worth reclaiming anyway.

Shaw had undergone a change in his attitude toward attempting to teach the common man, whether he be a rank-and-file Distributist or a rank-and-file Socialist. Despite his testy outburst to quiet down Titterton, G.B.S. did not mind much any more, as he would have ten years previously, that a personal appearance by him might add a few hundred dollars to the coffers of his theoretical enemies, the Distributists. For the poignant truth is that this was the time of life when the white-bearded Shaw was fast losing his confidence— except when dealing with a man of Chesterton's stature—that he could move people to positive action. As Marie Hochmuth Nichols has written: "Shaw undoubtedly lost some of his power over the middle classes somewhere in the twenties, when his speeches seemed to indicate that he himself had lost some faith in negotiation, compromise, constitutionalism, democracy,and perhaps, even common sense."[16]

G.B.S. may have entered the twilight of his career, but—brisk and efficient as ever—he had retained a full sense of the dignity and fitness of things. For example, once he had contracted for "Do We Agree?" G.B.S. did his best to insure that the Distributists would not transform the event into a fiasco. On October 20, 1927, he wrote to Chesterton insisting that the meeting be properly organized. It was quite evident, he said, that G.K.C.'s cronies in the Distributist League had no idea of what they were up against: "Nothing must be left to well-intentioned Godforsaken idiots, who have no experience or organizing power, and who believe that public meetings are a national phenomena that look after themselves. I'd rather pay Belloc's debts than get involved in something like that."[17]

Gregory Macdonald, the relatively competent secretary of the League, was in the process of hiring the huge Kingsway Hall for the debate when Shaw moved into the operation with a proprietary hand. G.B.S. approved Macdonald's action on Kingsway Hall and was even more pleased when Macdonald spoke of negotiating with the British Broadcasting Company to have the debate broadcast. Shaw, his business antennae reaching out, must have rubbed his hands together as he cautioned Macdonald: "Don't let them do you. Get a stiff fee. It's worth a hundred pounds to them to have Chesterton and me as a double turn."[18]

Inspired, Macdonald drove a hard bargain with the B.B.C. He won an agreement which stipulated that almost a full hundred pounds would be paid out to the Distributist League immediately after the debate had been broadcast. The money was not yet in hand, however; the League did not have a paid staff, and Macdonald faced an enormous task, inexperienced as he was, in arranging the actual details of the debate. Shaw took over. He did everything but set the last chair in place at Kingsway Hall. At first the old Socialist had been reluctant to take part in the venture at all. In the end he had so outdone himself for his friend that if the Distributists emerged solvent much would be owing to their foe, Bernard Shaw.

All the same a note of tension lingered among the younger Distributists on the afternoon of the debate. Some were wondering just how many people would bother to troop into the vast Kingsway Hall which it had cost them a considerable amount to rent. After all, Shaw was "ancient" and Chesterton was "elderly" even in the eyes of Titterton, who was no youth himself. Times had changed. The voices of Bright Young Things were clamoring on the London air for attention. Sensibility and Sophistication were the rages and young writers like Aldous Huxley and Evelyn Waugh were satisfying them. In the face of it all G.B.S.'s and G.K.C.'s continuing passions—for political, social, and economic justice—seemed cold and impersonal. Frankly, who cared in 1927 if Bernard Shaw, born in 1856, "agreed" with Gilbert Chesterton, born in 1874?

In the event, all London seemed to care. The young Distributists need not have worried. In fact the tumultuous attempts of crowds of people to storm Kingsway Hall on that November night to hear the old warriors debate must have seemed scarcely credible to the younger Distributists. Titterton gave a characteristically florid description of the event, and it is worth noting, for as Maisie Ward says, Titterton always "conveys in a unique way the Chestertonian atmosphere."[19]

> Despite our meagre means of advertisement, the great hall was packed long before the debate began. And throughout the proceedings wild hordes of men and women struggled in the corridors and hurled themselves against the shut doors of the hall. Once a door burst open, the shouts from outside became a pandemonium,

and the hot lava flowed down every alleyway. Then the door shut with a clang and the speakers could be heard again. I don't know how much of that was heard in the broadcast . . . it must have sounded like the outbreak of a revolution. Perhaps that was what it was.[20]

Years later Maisie Ward uncovered a witness who added corroborating detail:

There was an unrehearsed comedy as Belloc stood up to open the debate—roars from without, as of an angry multitude, followed by the clash of splintering glass and muffled cries of "Stop the debate!" The debate was being broadcast, so the doors had been shut very punctually, and the hall was packed. The riot (G.K. told us afterwards) was deliberately engineered by Ellis Roberts. He had arrived a minute or two late and was shut out with a crowd of other late-comers. He told G.K., "As a fat lady in diamonds was giving every indication of fainting on me, and as I had a ticket and had no intention of missing the fun, I just started a riot. It was a successful riot because they had to let us in to keep us quiet!"[21]

The unruly crowd sounds of that long ago night in 1927 make it appear particularly fortunate that Hilaire Belloc was the chairman of debate. Truculent old Hilary might have had his faults, but lack of authoritarian presence was not one of them. Belloc ruled the debate with a firm hand and a thumping gavel. The gavel brought to order not only the crowd but also G.B.S. and G.K.C. when either ventured (as both did) to speak beyond the allotted number of minutes.

Belloc also fulfilled a more important function than merely glowering or hammering a gavel. He both furthered and complemented the balanced literary tone which is the distinguishing mark of "Do We Agree?" Literary compliments to the debate tended to be isolated compliments paid to whichever speaker happened to be the particular favorite of a commentator. Yet the three men would seem to have deserved better for the blending of their three separate styles in "Do We Agree?" Once, Hesketh Pearson carefully classified Belloc as the Wit of Pugnacity, Shaw as the Wit of Criticism, and Chesterton as the Wit of Analogy.[22] Each produced splendid examples of these special qualities in "Do We Agree?"

As the Wit of Pugnacity, Belloc made his presence felt first. On the evening of the debate he had more reason than usual to be bellicose. He despised Socialism and considered Distributism useless. And he *was* Belloc! When he had an opinion, the world had to know it. Unlike most chairmen Belloc simply could not be expected to fade into the background and to hold his opinions to himself. As his friend Max Beerbohm said: "Hilary is a man of many geniuses but you know, he is something of a monomaniac."[23] In that context Belloc's introductory speech, which contained a famous combative conclusion, is quite understandable. On the night of the debate the speech did startle pleasantly an audience which had seemed incapable of being startled by anything:

> I am here to take the chair in the debate between two men whom you desire to hear more than you could possibly desire to hear me. They will debate whether they agree or do not agree. From what I know of attempts at agreement between human beings there is a prospect of a very pretty fight. When men debate agreements between nations then you may be certain a disastrous war is on the horizon. I make an exception for the League of Nations, of which I know nothing. If the League of Nations could make a war it would be the only thing it ever has made.
>
> I do not know what Mr. Chesterton is going to say. I do not know what Mr. Shaw is going to say. If I did I would not say it for them. I vaguely gather from what I have heard that they are going to try to discover a principle: Whether men should be free to possess private means, as is Mr. Shaw, as is Mr. Chesterton; or should be, like myself, an embarrassed person, a publishers'

hack. I could tell them; but my mouth is shut. I am not allowed to say what I think. At any rate, they are going to debate this sort of thing. I know not what more to say. They are about to debate. You are about to listen. I am about to sneer.[24]

Belloc had already overstepped his chairman role and established himself as a factor in the debate. All critics took his opening speech into account. Some quoted from it. Pearson noted that when Belloc had said "I am about to sneer," he had thrown "a savage glance at Shaw and resumed his seat."[25] William Irvine maintained that Belloc's opening remarks constituted the "most remarkable"[26] speech in the whole debate. Actually Belloc was to deliver a much better speech himself in the unorthodox summary he presented at the conclusion.

Shaw's opening address was also superior, a masterpiece of psychology, and the very epitome of G.B.S. speaking as the Wit of Criticism. Apparently Irvine missed the point of the Shavian art and purpose when he characterized this speech as "a scintillating conversation with himself about himself."[27] Shaw had been making use of a few comic opening remarks of self-aggrandizement as an attention getting device for forty years. Such mild braggadocio was a mere beginning, nothing more. Actually, the body of his opening speech in "Do We Agree?" contained perceptive critical remarks on the nature of his audience, on the methods of fiction which he and G.K.C. employed, on Socialism, on Distributism, on a whole panoply of subjects. Shaw's opening speech demonstrated that he had retained his passion to teach an audience as well as entertain it. G.B.S. kept his tones facetious only because such tones comported well with the rollicking nature of his audience. As Eric Bentley remarked: "What he says is always determined by the thought: what can I do to this audience? not by the thought: What is the most objective statement about this subject?"[28]

In the opening speech in "Do We Agree?" part of Shaw's purpose had been to wheedle, to cajole, or to coax his auditors into the conviction that he and G.K.C. were men of substance and that when conclusions had been found on which the two concurred, an audience had best heed those conclusions to its profit. The exposition of such a dry-as-dust purpose could have been tedious even in the hands of a good speaker. Witness Shaw as artist and Wit of Criticism achieve this aim in the most charming, indirect, and disarming manner possible:

> Mr. Chesterton tells and prints the most extravagant lies. He takes ordinary incidents of human life—commonplace middle-class life—and gives them a monstrous and strange and gigantic outline. He fills suburban gardens with the most impossible murders[29] and not only does he invent the murders but also succeeds in discovering the murderer who never committed the murders. I do very much the same sort of thing. I promulgate lies in the shape of plays; but whereas Mr. Chesterton takes events which you think ordinary and makes them gigantic and colossal to reveal their essential miraculousness, I am rather inclined to take these things in their utter commonplaceness, and yet to introduce among them outrageous ideas which scandalize the ordinary playgoer and send him away wondering whether he has been standing on his head all his life or whether I am standing on mine.
>
> A man goes to see one of my plays and sits by his wife. Some apparently ordinary thing is said on the stage, and his wife says to him: "Aha! What do you think of that?" Two minutes later another apparently ordinary thing is said and the man turns to his wife and says to her: "Aha! What do *you* think of *that*?"
>
> Curious, is it not, that we should go about doing these things and be tolerated and even largely admired for doing them? Of late years I might say that I have almost been reverenced for doing these things.

Obviously we are mad; and in the East we should be reverenced as madmen. The wisdom of the East says: "Let us listen to these men carefully; but let us not forget that they are madmen."

In this country they say "Let us listen to these amusing chaps. They are perfectly sane, which we obviously are not." Now there must be some reason for showing us all this consideration. There must be some force in nature which. . . .

At this point the debate was interrupted by persistent knocking at the doors by ticket-holders who had, through some misunderstanding, been locked out. On the chairman's intervention the doors were opened, and order was restored. Mr. Shaw then proceeded:

Ladies and Gentlemen, I must go on because, as you see, if I don't begin to talk everybody else does. Now I was speaking of the curious respect in which mad people are held in the East and in this country. What I was leading up to is this, that it matters very little on what points they differ: they have all kinds of aberrations which rise out of their personal circumstances, out of their training, out of their knowledge or ignorance. But if you listen to them carefully and find that at certain points they agree, then you have some reason for supposing that here the spirit of the age is coming through, and giving you an inspired message. Reject all the contradictory things they say and concentrate your attention on the things upon which they agree, and you may be listening to the voice of revelation.

You will do well to-night to listen attentively, because probably what is urging us to these utterances is not personal to ourselves but some conclusion to which all mankind is moving either by reason or by inspiration.

Shaw had taught the audience what he expected of it. In the process of teaching his lesson, he had managed to make warp and woof of such apparently irrelevant material as the

difference between his theory of fiction and G.K.C.'s. Along
the way G.B.S. had also been as entertaining and urbane as
any audience could wish. Yet he had postulated quite frankly
a noble and altruistic purpose. Now that he had made his purpose clear, he dropped at once the mask of G.B.S. as jester
and commenced his debate-long exposition of Socialism. He
made clear where his position on Socialism had changed since
1911. He cited an instance of social injustice which had
occurred not in the hoary past but a few days prior to the
debate. Considering his age, his performance in the debate
was remarkable, informed throughout by clarity and vigor.

Chesterton complemented both Belloc and Shaw. He,
too, preserved the bantering tone, the irony, and above all
the literary tone and allusions even as he entered into that
portion of the debate where he must inevitably disagree
with G.B.S.:

> So far, I say, you have Mr. Bernard Shaw and me walk-
> ing in fact side by side in the flowery meads. . . . But
> after that, alas! a change takes place. The change is ow-
> ing to Mr. Shaw's vast superiority, to his powerful intel-
> lect. It is not my fault if he has remained young, while
> I have grown in comparison wrinkled and haggard, old
> and experienced, and acquainted with the elementary
> facts of human life. . . . Mr. Shaw in his eternal youth
> . . . has even gone to the length of saying that if democ-
> racy will not do for mankind, perhaps it will do for some
> other creature different from mankind. He has almost
> proposed to invent a new animal which might be sup-
> posed to live for 300 years.[30] I am inclined to think that
> if Mr. Shaw lived for 300 years—and I heartily hope he
> will—I never knew a man more likely to do it—he
> would certainly agree with me. I would even undertake
> to prove it from the actual history of the last 300 years,
> but though I think it is probable I will not insist upon
> it. As a profound philosopher has said, "You never can
> tell." And it may be that Mr. Shaw's immortal power of

talking nonsense would survive even that 300 years and he would still be fixed in his unnatural theories in the matter.

Chesterton knew how to emulate the literary gambit of Shaw. Still, G.K.C. was best as the Wit of Analogy. Once in "Do We Agree?" Shaw cued beautifully a demonstration of G.K.C.'s precise use of analogy. At this point in the debate G.B.S. had been fulminating against the absolute powers of landlords in exercising the rights of ownership as opposed to the more properly limited use of power of ownership by the rest of us ordinary nonpropertied mortals. While establishing this thesis, he introduced a homely and apt analogy of his own to illustrate the point:

> I [when I act as a landlord] can take women in child-bearing and throw them into the snow and leave them there. That has been done. I can do it for no better reason than that I think it is better to shoot deer on the land than allow people to live on it. They might frighten the deer.
> But now compare that with the ownership of my umbrella. As a matter of fact the umbrella I have tonight belongs to my wife; but I think she will permit me to call it mine for the purpose of the debate. Now I have a very limited legal right to the use of that umbrella. I cannot do as I like with it. For instance, certain passages in Mr. Chesterton's speech tempted me to get up and smite him over the head with my umbrella. I may presently feel inclined to smite Mr. Belloc. But should I abuse my right to do what I like with my property—with my umbrella —in this way I should soon be made aware—possibly by Mr. Belloc's fist—that I cannot treat my umbrella as my own property in the way in which a landlord can treat his land. I want to destroy ownership in order that possession and enjoyment may be raised to the highest point in every section of the community. That, I think, is perfectly simple.

Shaw, as always seemed to happen when he produced a brilliant analogy of his own, sparked a brilliant response from Chesterton. Probably no one laughed louder than G.K.C. when G.B.S., dipping into the Chestertonian forte of wit by analogy, had created the spectacle of Belloc and himself being pummeled by Shaw's umbrella. At the same time G.K.C. recognized swiftly that, in so doing, Shaw had produced a fine statement of the problems involved in the twin doctrines of property and social freedom. G.K.C. decided to take a fling at appropriating the analogy to his own use:

> Among the bewildering welter of fallacies which Mr. Shaw has just given us, I prefer to deal first with the simplest. When Mr. Shaw refrains from hitting me over the head with his umbrella, the real reason—apart from his real kindness of heart, which makes him tolerant of the humblest of the creatures of God—is not because he does not own his umbrella, but because he does not own my head. As I am still in possession of that imperfect organ, I will proceed to use it to the confutation of some of his other fallacies.

G.K.C. had scored heavily with the audience by being able to project in a single line his own position on the question of property and social freedom. Chesterton would have been startled to learn that, later, critics would hint that Shaw must have "fed" him the line.[31] Until the end of the G.B.S.–G.K.C. relationship then, some men could not accept as true the speed and ease with which these men could thrust at and parry each other.

When the debate ended, Belloc delivered, instead of his scheduled summation, an instant appraisal of the debate in terms of its prospects for immortality. The prospects, he concluded, were nil. G.B.S. and G.K.C. had not been dealing with the stuff of immortality, for example, when the pair had disputed at length the relative merits of the collectivization of the coal industry in England. Such matters interested Belloc not at all. As always, he was willing to put on the record his own alternatives to what Shaw and Chesterton had prophesied. All Belloc's premonitions smacked of the voices of Xanadu prophesying war.

Still, Hilaire Belloc was interesting in his self-appointed role of Poet as Prophet. The gruff tone remained and that night the prophecy was gloomy. Yet many of Belloc's prejudices seemed to melt away when he relaxed into poetic concepts. He managed to convey the impression that while he disagreed with G.B.S. and G.K.C. to the end he was not without sympathy for the sincerity of their efforts:

> I was told when I accepted this onerous office that I was to sum up. I shall do nothing of the sort. In a very few years from now this debate will be antiquated. I will now recite you a poem:

> "Our civilization
> Is built upon coal.
> Let us chaunt in rotation
> Our civilization
> That lump of damnation
> Without any soul,
> Our civilization
> Is built upon coal.

> "In a very few years
> It will float upon oil.
> Then give three hearty cheers,
> In a very few years
> We shall mop up our tears
> And have done with our toil.
> In a very few years
> It will float upon oil."

In I do not know how many years—five, ten, twenty —this debate will be as antiquated as crinolines are. I am surprised that neither of the two speakers pointed out that one of three things is going to happen. One of three things: not one of two. It is always one of three things. This industrial civilization which, thank God, oppresses only the small part of the world in which we are most inextricably bound up, will break down and therefore end from its monstrous wickedness, folly, ineptitude, leading to a restoration of sane, ordinary human affairs, complicated but based as a whole upon the freedom of the citizens. Or it will break down and lead to nothing but a desert. Or it will lead the mass of men to become contented slaves, with a few rich men controlling them. Take your choice. You will all be dead before any of the three things comes off. One of the three things is going to happen, or a mixture of two, or possibly a mixture of the three combined.

Perhaps Belloc was right. New elaborations have replaced the forms of Socialism that G.B.S. sought to introduce. G.K.C.'s Distributism has long since been laid to rest as a solution. The advance of industrial civilization probably doomed peasant proprietorship before Chesterton was born. Belloc's melancholy comments even seem to suit better the modern literary mood. There is more of George Orwell's *1984* in what he said than in what G.B.S. or G.K.C. said.

Yet in a profound literary and political sense G.B.S. and G.K.C. pointed up in "Do We Agree?" principles of debate that are still of value. On that night in 1927 the debaters were able to send forth from Kingsway Hall an audience that was much better informed and less raucous although just as jovial as when it had entered. G.B.S. and G.K.C. had affected an audience on grave issues by a combination of wit, style, and analogy that both elevated and reassured. Today when platitudinous speech and platitudinous solution have more than ever failed to end violence one might explore the sane approach of a G.B.S. and G.K.C. with profit. At the least,

Shaw and Chesterton deserved this tribute to their methods
by Vincent Brome:

> So it went on. Not merely for this brief debate but for
> years. They agreed to differ in the most prolonged and
> eloquent way. If there were those who believed that
> neither could have very deep convictions and remain on
> such good terms, they overlooked not merely the com-
> mon humanity of both, but their ability to convince one
> another of this deeper identity. If there were those who
> suspected that the whole thing was rigged, that two
> theatrically minded authors had duped their audiences
> for the sake of sheer display, this was far removed from
> the civilized ideals both sought to serve.[32]

six

A NEW GLIMPSE OF *METHUSELAH*

The debates served as the raw material of art for G.B.S. and G.K.C. The Alpha of the raw material was often to be Socialism or Distributism. The Omega was always to be religion. No work demonstrated this better than Shaw's *Back to Methuselah* (1921). G.B.S. spoke his final word on Creative Evolution in *Methuselah,* and when he sat down to write it he was considering, among other things, the ideas and person of the G. K. Chesterton he had debated so often on the same subject.

Probably few can be surprised that G.K.C. had engaged in a lifelong dialogue on religion with G.B.S. For many readers G.K.C.'s Roman Catholic religion has become almost synonymous with his art. Possibly more readers would be surprised that a dialogue on religion with G.K.C. affected deeply a phase of Shaw's art. Somehow one did not associate G.B.S. with religion as quickly as one did G.K.C. Perhaps the reason was that the Shavian spiritual odyssey had infinitely more twists and turns than had G.K.C.'s relatively straight path to Rome.

All the same, Shaw was a genuinely religious man. His definitions of religion were so broad, unorthodox, and complex that as early as 1895 he was proposing to write a "gospel of Shawianity" to explain his religious history. Unfortunately, he never wrote it. Nevertheless, the material available on his religious position is enormous. Most of it is pertinent to

Methuselah and to the special area of the play where he intended to come to grips with G.K.C. as man and philosopher.

A summary of G.B.S.'s religious history is contained in his essay, "What Is My Religious Faith?"[1] Written when he was past ninety, it has the advantage of having been written as a work of clarification. In it one can travel with ease as G.B.S. goes past Darwin and Natural Selection, through Lamarckian Evolution, and up to his own brand of Creative Evolution. Shaw was never comfortable with Darwin because Natural Selection depended too much on blind chance. He seized happily on Lamarckian Evolution because Lamarck always postulated as a fundamental proposition that living organisms changed because they wanted to change. Actually, most of Lamarck's proposals dovetailed neatly with what G.B.S. hoped to achieve in his self-appointed role as artist-biologist. From Lamarck's stand, G.B.S. was able to formulate his own religion of Creative Evolution, in which he would dramatize Will, Life Force, and Voluntary Longevity as the scriptural aspects of his art. Always, the best and most subtle evidence of the maturation of Shaw's religious thought can be found in the plays. Outside the plays, Shaw deprecated his own original contributions to Creative Evolution. Instead he credited Henri Bergson and Bergson's *elan vital*[2] as "the established philosopher and philosophy of my sect." Further, G.B.S. called attention to Chevalier de Lamarck[3] as the scientist responsible for first elaborating an evolutionary process with "mind" in it. Generously, he would attribute the origin of many of his religious ideas to Bunyan, to Butler, or even to Bradlaugh, to Shelley, to Ibsen, to Voltaire, to the Gospel writers, or to many others. In Shaw's hands, however, the doctrines of Creative Evolution and the Life Force attained the stature of an original theology.

Man and Superman (1901–3) brought Shaw's religious position into focus, while *Back to Methuselah* (1921) saw its culmination. *Man and Superman* had failed to clear the air on his religious position, although G.B.S. had hoped that it would: "I had always known that civilization needs a religion as a matter of life or death; and as the conception of Creative Evolution developed, I saw that we were at last within reach of a faith which complied with the first condition of all the religions that have ever taken hold of humanity: namely, that it must be, first and fundamentally, a science of metabiology. . . . Accordingly, in 1901, I took the legend of Don Juan, in its Mozartian form and made it a dramatic parable of Creative Evolution."[4] But Shaw failed to clarify his theology in *Man and Superman,* and he afterwards knew why: "But being then at the height of my invention and comedic talent, I decorated it too brilliantly and lavishly. I surrounded it with a comedy of which it formed only one act. . . . Also I supplied the published work with an imposing framework consisting of a preface, an appendix called The Revolutionist's Handbook, and a final display of aphoristic fireworks. The effect was so vertiginous, apparently, that nobody noticed the new religion in the centre of the intellectual whirlpool."[5] A generation later G.B.S. proposed to remedy the situation by making his final statement on Creative Evolution in *Back to Methuselah.*

> I now find myself inspired to make a second legend of Creative Evolution without distractions and embellishments. My sands are running out; the exuberance of 1901 has aged into the garrulity of 1920. . . . I abandon the legend of Don Juan with its erotic associations, and go back to the legend of the Garden of Eden. I exploit the eternal interest of the philosopher's stone which enables men to live forever. I am not, I hope, under more illusion . . . as to the crudity of this my beginning of the Bible for Creative Evolution. I am doing the best I can at my age. . . . It is my hope that a hundred apter and more elegant parables by younger hands will soon

leave mine . . . far behind. . . . In that hope I withdraw
and ring up the curtain.[6]

A Metabiological Pentateuch, *Back to Methuselah* was
an overwhelming work in every sense. One aspect that overwhelmed was its prolixity and inordinate length. Another was
its time span. G.B.S. provided in *Methuselah* a historical
treatment of religion which extended from "In the Beginning:
B.C. 4004 (In the Garden of Eden)" to "As Far as Thought
Can Reach: A.D. 31,920." Chesterton was to write: "This
business about Creative Evolution noted in my book under
the name and topic of *Man and Superman* has since taken a
much longer stride in the work called *Back to Methuselah*.
It is a very long stride indeed for the play lasts for two or
three nights, as if to prepare its audience for the practice of
living for two or three hundred years."[7]

G.K.C.'s comment contained substance. Yet, G.B.S.
must have been amused that G.K.C., of all people, had
launched one of the attacks on the Shavian scriptural edifice.
For G.K.C. happened to possess, unawares, an integral relationship to the very composition of *Back to Methuselah*.
G.B.S. had kept this fact an intriguing literary secret from
1921, when he published the play, until 1931, when he
revealed that he had written additional material for it, as yet
unpublished. The material had been for an act in the part of
the play titled "The Gospel of the Brothers Barnabas." In
1932, G.B.S. finally did publish this 45-page act under its
own title, "A Glimpse of the Domesticity of Franklyn Barnabas."[8] When at last the Shavian secret became public knowledge, Chesterton himself, disguised thinly as Immenso Champernoon, emerged before the public as the major character
of "Domesticity"!

Actually Shaw had intended to divide Part II of *Methuselah* into two acts, the present "Gospel of the Brothers Bar-

nabas" and "The Domesticity of Franklyn Barnabas," later discarded. G.B.S.'s script for the two acts—written in his inimitable Pitman shorthand—is still on view in the British Museum. He had begun "Gospel" on March 19, 1918, and completed his first draft of it on April 9, 1918. When he began to write "Domesticity," is not clear, although obviously it was after April 9, but G.B.S. does give a completion date for "Domesticity," November 12, 1918, the day after World War I ended.

In composing his religious testament G.B.S. had found it impossible to ignore the friend and rival who had defended the traditional concepts of religion against him for so many years. Indeed, Immenso Champernoon-Chesterton had gotten out of hand. Shaw's modest plans for him had gone awry when Immenso developed into a dynamic character who might have destroyed the balance of the play. H. M. Geduld wrote,[9] in effect, that Immenso Champernoon is an overwhelming character to whom the fragment of a play is attached. It is not, claimed Geduld, difficult to see that Champernoon was the major reason why Shaw discarded the "Domesticity" piece. If Immenso had imposed his bulk on Burge and Lubin, the resulting comedy would have become unbalanced, and Shaw would have been forced into redirecting later segments.

In truth Shaw had discarded Immenso and "Domesticity" for two reasons. First, Shaw's prime motive had been to keep his biological drama on straight rails. G.B.S. had refused to permit anyone, even his protagonist Franklyn Barnabas, let alone Champernoon, to distract his audience from the theme of *Methuselah*. As G.B.S. explained it: "It was with this thesis of the Barnabases that I was concerned when I wrote *Back to Methuselah;* and though I got interested enough in Franklyn personally to go a little way into his domestic history, I had to discard my researches as both irrelevant and certain to sidetrack my main theme and confuse my biological drama with a domestic comedy."[10]

In Shaw's view Franklyn Barnabas, the ex-clergyman, and his brother Conrad, the biologist, would have been badgered comically by officious Clara (Franklyn's wife), beguiling Rosie Etteen (Franklyn's paramour), and the impossible Immenso Champernoon (Franklyn's brother-in-law). In domestic comedy Franklyn and Conrad would have been hard put to expound with dignity the theory that once scientists had extended the range of life to three hundred years, man, as a Long Liver, must pursue noble ends because he could no longer find retreat in that age-old excuse of Short Livers, "Let us eat and drink; for tomorrow we die."

Ironically, Shaw gave as the second reason for discarding "Domesticity" the opinion that his attempt to re-create Chesterton as Immenso had resulted in artistic failure. As G.B.S. put it: "I had amused myself by bringing Franklyn Barnabas into contact with a notable social philosopher of our day for the mere fun of caricaturing him. But this proved a hopeless enterprise; for, like all really great humorists, he had himself exploited his own possibilities so thoroughly in that direction that I could produce nothing but a manifestly inferior copy of a gorgeous original."

Shaw was wrong. Critics were generally agreed that G.B.S. had performed a marvel of mimicry with Immenso Champernoon. In temperament, in physique, in mannerism, in flashing gifts of analogy and intellect, Immenso is G.K.C. to the life. G.B.S. even brought Immenso on to the stage with as fine a thumb nail portrait of Chesterton as exists: *"Immenso Champernoon is a man of colossal mould with the head of a cherub on the body of a Falstaff, which he carries with ease and not without grace. At forty or thereabouts his hair is still brown and curly. He is friendly, a little shy, and jokes frequently enough to be almost always either still*

*enjoying the last or already anticipating the next. He is care-
less of his dress and person, in marked contrast to Franklyn,
who, though untidy as to his papers, looks comparatively
valeted and manicured."*

From the outset all critics found something in which to
delight in G.B.S.'s characterization of his friend. On the other
hand, praise for the playlet was by no means universal. In
fact a first reading of "Domesticity" could lead easily to this
critic's conclusion:

> "A Glimpse into the Domesticity of Franklyn Barnabas"
> . . . introduces Chesterton as Immenso Champernoon
> into a hornets' nest of Shavian vitalists. This dialogue
> is a wonderful little reproduction of his generous outer
> husk in violent and comic motion. Champernoon trans-
> forms himself into a Highland Chief with a traveling
> rug, does medieval battle with a golf stick, drums out
> "The Campbells are Coming" with a dinner gong, and
> delivers himself into the hands of a Shavian sibyl with
> speeches that set ablaze elaborate filaments of Chester-
> tonian wit, paradox, and wordplay in an almost com-
> plete vacuum of sense. With a devastating brilliance
> Shaw proves that the style is not the man. But the dia-
> logue goes beyond travesty. It is a patronizing puritan's
> indictment of a cavalier. The Shavian sibyl is good-
> natured, indulgent, and often sound. In fact, she does
> everything but take Champernoon seriously and grants
> him everything but a point of view.[11]

Yet quite the reverse was true. The sibyl, Rosie Etteen, had
not only granted Champernoon-Chesterton a point of view
but had spent a good part of the act urging Immenso to
express that point of view explicitly. Naturally, G.B.S. had
made "Domesticity" a showcase for his own ideas. But this
did not prevent Shaw the artist from granting Immenso several telling and brilliant speeches.

Shaw accomplished even more with Champernoon-
Chesterton. One could learn a lesson in integrity from the

manner in which G.B.S. handled the caricature of his friend. G.B.S. had Champernoon-Chesterton engage in dialogue only when he could affirm Chestertonian principles or perform some action consistent with those principles. Shaw did not put cheap lines into Immenso's mouth to belie the actual Chestertonian positions on institutions sacred to him, such as marriage. For example, at one point in the dialogue Immenso is hovering in the background when Franklyn's wife Clara cites to his paramour, Rosie Etteen, her reason for remaining loyal to husband, home, and children: "But they belong here and I belong here; and you dont,[12] darling; and thats what makes all the difference." Immediately Shaw makes Immenso drop all circumlocutions to add with dignity: "I think that settles it, Mrs. Etteen."

Again, when Conrad, the biologist, attempts to make a joke about Immenso's size, he founders on a wave of superior comment by Champernoon. In real life no man could make better jokes about his size than could G.K.C. Shaw had kept his portrait of Chesterton accurate even as to detail.

On the other hand, G.B.S. was just as quick to censure Immenso when he deserved it. Franklyn complains at once when he traps Champernoon "playing with his mind" or mixing metaphors. In real life G.K.C. was prone to both faults. When a character in the playlet criticizes a gaff by Immenso, one can be reasonably certain that the real-life Chesterton was likely to make the same sort of gaff.

Shaw was careful to keep his characterization precise on the larger issues, too. Immenso bested Conrad (the biologist) in debate because Conrad was a static representative of pure science and the Life Force. Conversely, the alluring Mrs. Rosie Etteen represented quite a different challenge for Immenso. Mrs. Etteen as artist-musician ranked high in the Shavian hierarchy of values. Therefore, G.B.S. tricked her out in the playlet as the most subtle practitioner of the theory of the Life Force. Only Mrs. Etteen seemed able to equal or best Champernoon in debate.

The question that overrides the playlet is whether or not Rosie Etteen did best Immenso Champernoon in debate. Opinions vary in the extreme. William Irvine, for example, was convinced that Mrs. Etteen had been permitted to make a travesty of Champernoon-Chesterton. Shaw, however, seems to have been scrupulously fair to Chesterton. Actually, neither Immenso nor Rosie is a clear-cut victor in the debate. It had been toward this duel-debate between Rosie as arch vitalist of the Life Force and Immenso as the lay priest of common sense that Shaw had been pointing his playlet all along. Cleverly, G.B.S. makes Mrs. Etteen the immediate cause of conflict as well as the ultimate advocate of the Life Force. Rosie is lovely, thrice divorced, and an intimate enough friend of Franklyn to cause his wife Clara discomfort. In fact, Clara becomes so irritated that she deserts Franklyn for a week and is just returning to hearth and board as the playlet opens. At first Clara is not exactly overjoyed to have Immenso available to do battle for her as champion of the Christian approach in settling family disputes. Clara herself favors Karma, Yoga, Reincarnation, or any religious succour rooted in the East. Nevertheless, her attitude changes when Franklyn proves intractable and her marital difficulties reach an impasse. Gradually she becomes willing to enlist Immenso as intermediary with Franklyn to protect her family interests. When Immenso finally arrives at the Barnabas household he is indeed quite alone as champion of Christian family solidarity. The "hornets' nest of vitalists" is assembled. Conrad, Franklyn, Rosie, Haslam, the young curate, Savvy, Clara's daughter—are all there. Clara more or less introduces Immenso to Rosie Etteen:

MRS. ETTEEN: . . . Is this your famous brother, Mr. Immenso Champernoon?

*Immenso, who has been sitting as if mesmerized, too
shy to look at anyone, starts convulsively to his feet and
presents himself for inspection with his hands hanging
limply at his sides and his eyes directed to the carpet.*

CLARA: Yes: thats Immenso. He's no use to you: he's
happily married. Imm: this is Mrs. Etteen.

IMMENSO: [*murmuring thunderously*] Ahooroo. Eh Plea.
[*He is understood to have said "How do you do? Very
pleased." They shake hands.*]

CLARA: Doctor Conrad Barnabas, Franklyn's brother.
Unmarried. Fair game; so he wont interest you.

MRS. ETTEEN: You are very naughty, Clara. How do
you do, Doctor? I have read your book [*shaking
hands*].

CONRAD: How do you do?

CLARA: I can be quite as candid as you, Rosie darling.
Sure youve had tea?

MRS. ETTEEN: Quite. [*She sits down next Immenso and
turns her eyes full on him*]. Mr. Champernoon: you
are the wisest man in England when you are not talking glorious nonsense. Can you explain something to
me?

IMMENSO: [*trying to recover his assurance in the dangerous warmth of the violet eyes*] Explanation is not a
difficult art. I should say that any fool can explain
anything. Whether he can leave you any the wiser is
another matter.

MRS. ETTEEN: Would you believe that I have been married three times?

IMMENSO: Does that need an explanation? Have you not
such a thing in your house as a mirror?

MRS. ETTEEN: Oh! Gallant! You make me blush.

Happily for admirers of Shavian caricature and portraiture, G.B.S. refused to make Rosie and Immenso settle down
to debate at once. Instead Rosie employs her considerable
charm to delude an all-too-human Champernoon into believing that although she loves Franklyn, she is now trying to
fascinate him. Immenso's reaction is to play the gallant, and

once the mood of gallantry is established, he yields to it completely. Mrs. Etteen is somewhat nettled at Immenso's knightly stance because her real purpose is to engage the unsuspecting Champernoon in a serious argument on the Life Force. Yet for reasons of strategy she is willing to satisfy up to a point her foil's penchant for gallantry and revelry.

Clara is delighted with the turn of events. Anxious to keep Franklyn from Rosie, she helps steer the action so that Mrs. Etteen is forced more than ever to cater to Immenso's whims. Shaw employs all three characters to create a pleasant clamor of action on the stage. The action is again consistent with that of the real Chesterton who exulted in horseplay although his convivial companions tended to be men, and in the playlet his companion is to be the ultra-feminine Rosie Etteen:

> CLARA: Savvy: take Rosie and Imm to the drawing room; and let us have some music. Imm hasnt heard Rosie play; and the sooner he gets it over, the better.
> MRS. ETTEEN: [*moving towards the door*] Do you really want any music, Mr. Champernoon?
> IMMENSO: [*going with her*] In moods of battle and victory I want the bagpipes, Mrs. Etteen. My wife imitates them on the black keys of the piano. I do the drum, with a dinner gong. [*They go out.*]
>
> .   .   .   .
>
> HASLAM: Rather a lark it would be, wouldnt it, if Uncle Imm were to cut Mr Barnabas out with Mrs. Etteen?
> CLARA: Imm has no ear for music. She cant do it with the piano anyhow.[13]
> *A hollow chord of G flat and D flat is heard droning from the drawing room piano. Then The Campbells are Coming is played on the black keys.*
> *A drum obbligato begins on the dinner gong, played at first with childish enjoyment, and proceeding, in a rapid crescendo, to ecstasy.*
> HASLAM: She is doing it with the piano! Priceless!

CLARA: [*indignantly*] Well!

SAVVY: [*rushing in*] Mother: do come and stop Uncle Imm. If he starts dancing he will shake the house down. Oh, listen to them. [*She puts her fingers in her ears.*]

CLARA: [*rushing out*] Stop, stop! Imm! Rosie! Stop that horrible noise.

SAVVY: [*shutting the door with a slam*] Did you ever hear anything like it? Uncle Imm is the greatest baby.

The noise suddenly stops with the sound of the dinner gong being torn from Imm's grasp and flung down on the carpet, presumably by Clara. The piano takes the hint and stops too. . . . The dinner gong is heard bumping against something outside. . . . Immenso enters in the character of a Highland chieftain carrying the gong like a target, and a hockey stick like a claymore. He had heightened the illusion by draping his shoulder with a travelling rug. He marches about, humming The Campbells. *Mrs. Etteen follows, half annoyed, half amused, and sits down on the sofa.*

SAVVY: [*still excited, to Immenso*] Sillybilly, sillybilly, sillybilly! Fat boy of Peckham! [*She snatches a ruler from the writing table. Immenso disposes himself immediately for combat. She makes a feint which he utterly fails to parry, and stabs him with the ruler. He falls ponderously and cautiously.*] Slain! Slain! Mrs. Etteen will receive your last breath. Come Bill. [*She runs out.*]

HASLAM: Priceless! [*He runs out after her.*]

IMMENSO: [*rising with difficulty*] "Unwounded from the dreadful close; but breathless all, Fitzjames arose."

MRS. ETTEEN: Mr. Champernoon: would you mind growing up for a moment; and condescending to treat me as an adult person?

IMMENSO: If you insist on our keeping up that dreary affectation I am bound to obey you. [*He throws down the hockey stick, the rug, and finally the gong.*] Farewell, ye real things. How good it is to hear your solid thump on the floor! The human boy sleeps with you there. The literary gasbag floats gently to your feet, madam. [*He sits down on the chair furthest away from her.*]

Immenso realizes that he has been tapped for serious conversation. Nevertheless, he is still smug in the conviction that the only topic on the agenda is to be romantic love. Immenso does not seem to have the slightest intimation that he is falling into the snare of a rampant Life-Forcer. At first Mrs. Etteen is not inclined to disenchant him. She begins circuitously, putting forth advanced ideas on love and marriage that are Shavian in essence but not so overtly Shavian that Immenso is able to diagnose them properly. In fact, Immenso is blithely parrying Mrs. Etteen with all the aplomb of a professional moralist when she administers to him the first of a series of shocks:

> MRS. ETTEEN: [*with dignity*] Mr. Champernoon: is it possible that you think I am discussing the question of sex with you?
> IMMENSO: [*taken aback*] Well—er— Well, good heavens! what else are we discussing!
> MRS. ETTEEN: *I* am discussing beauty, which is not a matter of taste at all, but a matter of fact as to which no difference of opinion is possible among cultivated people. Can you produce a single person of any culture who thinks the Venus of Milo or the Hermes of Praxiteles ugly? Can you produce a single person who thinks—
> IMMENSO: Who thinks me beautiful? Not one.

The resort to quip proves only that Immenso is on the run. He is obviously embattled. The real G.K.C. also had the habit of resorting to jest when danger signals warned him to press for time and advantage. In this instance, however, Rosie

Etteen is not to be denied. She levels a blast of Shavianism full upon the hapless Champernoon:

> MRS. ETTEEN: I have seen worse, Mr. Champernoon. [*He bows*] You are very like Balzac, of whom Rodin made one of the greatest statues in the world. But dont you see that this sex attraction, though it is so useful for keeping the world peopled, has nothing to do with beauty. . . . You can do without the Venus of Milo because the young lady at the refreshment bar can make you forget her. I dont want to talk about such attractions: they are only the bait in the trap of marriage: they vanish when they have served their turn. But have you never known really beautiful people, beautiful as girls, beautiful as matrons, beautiful as grandmothers, or men to match them? Do you not want a world of such beautiful people, instead of what the gentleman in Mr. Granville-Barker's play calls "this farmyard world of sex"? Will you dare to tell me that the world was no worse when the lords of creation were monkeys than it is now that they are men, ugly as most of them are?

The conversation has changed into debate. The beleaguered Champernoon does make a last feeble effort to divert Rosie into humorous channels but Mrs. Etteen holds firm, refusing any longer to play the role of coquette. Instead she presses Champernoon inexorably:

> MRS. ETTEEN: No: you shall not ride off on a quip, Mr. Champernoon. Stand to your guns. You thought I was going to entice you into a flirtation: you see now that I am trying to convert you to a religion of beauty.
> IMMENSO: I am not sure that I do not think you all the more dangerous. You might pervert me intellectually; but on the other ground, I am invincible. I cannot flirt. I am not what is called a lady's man, Mrs. Etteen.

Immenso's smug declaration that he is not a flirt infuriates Mrs. Etteen. She proceeds to make a personal attack on Champernoon in terms that repeat point by point the terms of the personal attack that G.B.S. had made upon G.K.C. in the drawing room in Chelsea in 1923. The difference between the attack in Chelsea and the attack in "Domesticity" is that a cool and controlled Bernard Shaw edited the "Domesticity" version in 1931, nine years after the fact of G.K.C.'s conversion to the Roman Catholic Church. Oddly, the touch of moderation and control so evident in the writing makes the piece a more effective skewering of Champernoon-Chesterton than had been the tirade in Chelsea. G.B.S. had managed, whether consciously or unconsciously, to translate the substance of a spontaneous debate with G.K.C. into the medium of his art:

> MRS. ETTEEN: You cannot flirt! Mr. Champernoon: you are the most incorrigible flirt in England, and the very worst sort of flirt too. You flirt with religions, with traditions, with politics, with everything that is most sacred and important. You flirt with the Church, with the Middle Ages, with the marriage question, with the Jewish question, even with the hideous cult of gluttony and drunkenness. Every one of your discussions of these questions is like a flirtation with a worthless woman: you pay her the most ingenious and delightful compliments, driving all your legitimate loves mad with distress and jealousy; but you are not a bit in earnest: behind all your sincere admiration of her priceless pearls and her pretty paint you loathe the creature's flesh and blood. You are all flirts, you intellectuals. If you flirted with housemaids and dairymaids, or with chorus girls, I could forgive you; but to flirt with ghastly old hags because they were the mistresses of kings and of all the oppressors of the earth is despicable and silly.

The fencing is over. At last Mrs. Etteen is attacking Champernoon with words that draw blood and words that demand counterattack. From this point on the dialogue remains earnest:

> IMMENSO: [*reddening*] I deny that innuendo. I was in a Liberal set, a Protestant set, an atheist set, a Puritan set. I had everything to lose by defending the Church and the Middle Ages, by denouncing Puritanism, by affirming the existence of God.
>
> . . . .
>
> Why do I uphold the Church: I, who know as much of the crimes of the Churches as you do? Not for what the Church did for men, but for what men did for the Church. It brought us no gifts; but it drew forth gifts from us. And that is just as it should be. I love the Church because Michelangelo painted its churches. You complain of it because the churches did not paint Michelangelo. Well, suppose they had painted him! Suppose they had tarred and feathered him! Would you not place the painting of Michelangelo, with the burning of John Huss or Giordano Bruno or Joan of Arc, among the crimes of the Churches?

In this speech Shaw had provided the Champernoon-Chesterton character a legitimate point of view. G.B.S. had provided Immenso a better retort to Rosie than G.K.C. himself had been able to frame for Shaw in the drawing room debate in Chelsea. The Christian axiom "It is better to give than to receive" could scarcely have received a sounder application than when Champernoon-Chesterton argued that in relation to the Church even a Michelangelo should expect to give of his art rather than to receive.

On the other hand, Shaw had not relinquished his own convictions. He permits Champernoon-Chesterton to join the battle fairly, but he is not necessarily going to see to it that Immenso wins the battle. This is, after all, a debate. Mrs. Etteen is provided full opportunity to flare back in kind:

> MRS. ETTEEN: That is a very pretty little juggle with words, and very funny. But when you are talking of Michelangelo you are talking of a man so great that he was literally a demigod. When you talk of the Church, you are talking of a pack of common men calling themselves clergymen and priests, trying to persuade us that they are demigods by wearing ugly black clothes. Michelangelo did not paint for them: he painted for me, and for people like you and me. We are the spectators for whom he painted: we are the Church which drew out his gifts. It was for us that Bach and Beethoven composed, that Phidias and Rodin made statues, that the poets sang and the philosophers became seers. It is you who are faithless and disloyal in giving the allegiance we owe to them to corrupt gangs of little lawyers and politicians and priests and adventurers organized as States and Churches and dressed up like actors to seem the thing they are not. They pretend to see events with glass eyes, and to hear the music of the spheres with ass's ears. [*She pauses. Immenso is staring before him like a man in a trance.*] Are you listening? [*He does not answer.*] I know. You are thinking how you can work all this into an article.
>
> IMMENSO: [*waking up suddenly*] Damn it, I am.[14] [*He salutes.*] Touché!

Then Rosie Etteen makes a fateful slip. In urging Champernoon to rise to revolutionary action rather than to content himself with magazine articles, she reveals that she is indeed an apostle of Creative Evolution, a zealot of the religion of the Life-Force. The fact stuns Immenso. At last he is irrevocably aware that this seductive creature has led him *Back to Methuselah*. Immenso is to manage only a single shout of indignation before Mrs. Etteen documents for him her exalted rank in the hierarchy of Creative Evolution:

> IMMENSO: [*starting*] What! Are you on this Back-to-Methuselah tack too? Has all this been the craze of my brothers-in-law at second hand?
>
> MRS. ETTEEN: Oh, very manly man that you are, it does not occur to you that Franklyn Barnabas may have had this from me. Did he ever speak of it before he met me?
>
> IMMENSO: Now that you mention it, no. But it began with Conrad; and you certainly did not work in his laboratory.
>
> MRS. ETTEEN: Conrad never saw the scope of his idea any more than Weismann, from whom he got it. He saw how it affected science: he knew that he had to die when he was just beginning to discover what science really is, and had just found out that the experience of people who die at seventy is only a string of the mistakes of immaturity. He had the skeleton of the great faith; but it was Franklyn who put the flesh on it. And it was I, the woman, who made that flesh for him out of my own. That is my relation to Franklyn. That is what Clara would call the intrigue between us.

Clearly Rosie Etteen had emerged as the most articulate advocate of the Life-Force in "The Domesticity of Franklyn Barnabas." Actually the debate between Rosie and Immenso did not persist much longer and its conclusion was markedly tentative. Shaw was shrewd enough not to adjudge a victor. He wrote: "How this conversation ended I cannot tell; for I never followed up the adventure of Immenso Champernoon with Mrs. Etteen, and dont believe it came to anything."

The general felicity of the Champernoon-Chesterton character and the spirited debating match between Rosie and Immenso have combined to make "Domesticity" essential material for Shaw-Chesterton study. On its own terms the domestic comedy contained still another feature worthy of note. One can find almost every concept of the Shavian religion buried in "Domesticity." Unfortunately, this rather interesting fact has led to an extravagant claim or two for the playlet. On March 6, 1960, "Domesticity" gained one of its rare public hearings, moving critic Arthur Gelb to write the next day in *The New York Times:* "As a matter of fact the little-known domestic comedy, as read informally and entertainingly in the Grolier Club library Sunday night under the auspices of The Shaw Society of America, does more to advance the cause of Creative Evolution and of Shavianism than its windy parent work. 'A Glimpse of Domesticity' contains, succinctly and funnily, the nucleus of the *Back to Methuselah* philosophy; unless a man learns (by applying the Barnabas theory of Creative Evolution) how to extend his life span to 300 years, he is destined to extinction."[15]

Gelb's claim was extreme. Shavians might justly deny that the one-act domestic comedy did "more to advance the cause of Creative Evolution and Shavianism than its windy parent work." "Domesticity" does no such thing. G.B.S., writing for publication in 1921, needed more than the forty-five pages of "Domesticity" to serve as platform for the new philosophy of Creative Evolution. Ideas like Life Force and Voluntary Longevity were then sounding on unaccustomed ears. How could G.B.S. have satisfied an audience with an outline playlet in which many of his ideas were only implicit? Even the longer *Man and Superman* (1901) had failed to accomplish Shaw's purpose. G.B.S. himself had admitted that although *Superman* had contained many of the same concepts, he had packaged the ideas too entertainingly so that he lost reflective audiences on a wave of levity. He resolved not to make the same mistake with *Methuselah.*

First, he took care to make *Methuselah* more sober and solemn than *Superman.* Then he employed repetition as the

staple of his literary method in order to make the doctrine of
Creative Evolution ineluctably clear. The approach seemed
sound enough. Writers have always depended upon rhythmic
repetitions and elaborations to propound serious themes. Yet
Methuselah has failed to achieve first rank as a work of art
or entertainment. G.B.S. had lost classic restraint. He had
allowed his script to grow overlong and the number of his
repetitions to become excessive. G.B.S. had finally achieved
clarity for his theme of Creative Evolution but at the price
of art. Nevertheless, *Methuselah* did not misfire completely
and G.B.S. needed each of his characters, Burge, Lubin, The
Elderly Gentleman—the whole complement—to embody
theatrically his concept of Creative Evolution. Yet *Methuselah* needed Immenso, too. Shaw might legitimately have
retained "Domesticity" as part of the parent work, adding to
the attractiveness of *Methuselah* as art and entertainment.
"Domesticity" was more than an excellent piece of work in
itself. The playlet was so constructed that it had the potential
to increase the integral value of *Methuselah*. Minor characters like Franklyn and Conrad, so flat in *Methuselah,* take
on flesh and blood and come alive only in the rejected fragment. Even the briefer characterizations of Rosie Etteen and
Clara Barnabas are good enough to deserve a niche in the
play. Yet Immenso is the key. The Champernoon-Chesterton
characterization is art. Whether or not Immenso took on
such strength and authenticity because he was based upon a
human model or because he appeared in the warm confines
of domestic comedy, Champernoon-Chesterton did gain a
dimension of humanity and plausibility denied other characters in *Methuselah.*

On the whole "Domesticity" succeeded in fulfilling the
elusive requirements of both art and entertainment. When
Immenso cavorted, the comedy managed to present the Shavian doctrines in palatable and entertaining form. One also

makes the pleasant discovery that in the playlet G.B.S., while caricaturing G.K.C., had been unable to resist poking fun at his own sacred theory of Creative Evolution. Apparently, even when G.B.S. or G.K.C. merely wrote about one another, the sane perspective that humor provides was never too far away.

Speculation cannot change the fact that Shaw, who had good reasons of his own, saw fit to expunge "Domesticity" from the final version of his play. Happily the domestic comedy has managed to survive on its own terms. A charming adjunct to the study of *Methuselah,* "Domesticity" can also hold its own as an entertaining primer for the parent work because it does contain the nucleus of the Shavian ideas on Creative Evolution. Finally, "Domesticity" does seem absolutely secure as a repository for Shaw-Chesterton study.

One intriguing fact about the playlet remains to be examined. Shaw had been firmly convinced that "Domesticity" impeded the theme of *Methuselah* and that his portrait of G.K.C. as Immenso had been an artistic failure. Why then did G.B.S. decide in 1931 that it would be useful, after all, to publish the playlet? Fortunately, G.B.S. went on the record with two reasons for his decision to publish "Domesticity." The first may disconcert Chestertonians who think that every move involving their idol should be motivated only by desire to place him among the immortals. The truth is that Shaw published "Domesticity" first because, in searching about his study for material to pad out *Scraps and Shavings,* he found the discarded act and thought it would help to fulfill that humble function nicely. On the other hand, G.B.S.'s second reason may bolster up and give heart to Chestertonians:

> Still, even a bad caricature may have some value when the original has dissolved into its elements for remanufacture by the Life Force. As we cannot now have a photograph of Shakespear, much less a portrait by a master, we cling to the inhuman caricature by Droeshout

as at least a corrective to the commonplace little bust of a commonplace little gent in the shrine in Stratford church; and so I think it possible that my thumbnail sketch, inadequate and libellous as it is, may give a hint or two to some future great biographer as to what the original of Immenso Champernoon was like in the first half of his career, when, in defiance of the very order of nature, he began without a figure as a convivial immensity with vine leaves in his hair, deriding his own aspect, and in middle life slimmed into a Catholic saint, thereby justifying my reminder to those who took him too lightly of old, that Thomas Aquinas began as a comically fat man and ended as The Divine Doctor.

Despite his facetious overtones, G.B.S. was completely sincere in this descriptive evaluation of G.K.C. He believed first and last that Chesterton was a man of genius. In creating Champernoon-Chesterton, G.B.S. had found himself trying to reproduce a measure of that genius on paper. His verbal portrait of his friend was unpretentious, and G.B.S., having cut it from the play, was in the position of having composed it only for the amusement it afforded him. Nevertheless, the portrait happens to be vivid in detail and handsome in sweep—clearly the best characterization of Chesterton that exists. Until Immenso has received his tithe of glory, no honorable revival of G.K.C. could ever be considered complete.

seven

THE LAST PHASE, 1928–36

To evaluate the effects of the Shaw-Chesterton relationship, one must understand what the relationship was and what it was not. The standard characterization of the relationship as a lifelong friendship and controversy combined is not quite accurate. Only the friendship was lifelong. Active controversy ended in 1928, eight years before G.K.C.'s death. This fact can be significant in evaluating effects. The end to decades of written and oral debate seemed to come quite suddenly. Late in 1927, publisher Cecil Palmer had handed to G.B.S. and to G.K.C. for approval the proofs of the speeches in the debate "Do We Agree?" The two men edited the speeches carefully. Each made a number of revisions and emendations before returning the proofs. In 1928 Palmer published the debate as the book *Do We Agree?* The little book proved popular and quickly ran through several printings. After more than two decades, the Shaw-Chesterton controversy could still attract a public.

Then, as suddenly as with Browning's "Last Duchess," all smiles and arguments seemed to stop altogether. No more public debates occurred. No new G.B.S.–G.K.C. anecdotes appeared to lend a dash of color to the literary landscape. Literary exchanges ceased. What had happened? It is true that the literary side of the relationship did not disappear completely. For example, in 1935, at the instigation of his publishers, G.K.C. did add a substantial chapter, "The Later Phases," to his early book on Shaw. The chapter was significant (and will be referred to again) but it was not controversial in the old G.B.S.–G.K.C. sense of attack and counterattack. Years later G.B.S. was to edit for Maisie Ward her summary of the G.B.S.–G.K.C. relationship. But that was about all. After 1928 no new controversy flared up. Moreover, personal contact between the two friends dwindled more than even Shaw's world cruises or G.K.C.'s two teaching tours at Notre Dame, Indiana, would seem to warrant. Again, the question arises: What had happened?

No act of hostility had occurred. The record of 1928–36 reveals only an occasional reference of one to the other, but the reference is always affectionate. In the thirties, when he had but a year or two to live, G.K.C. told a worried Canadian seminarian, who had asked whether Bernard Shaw was a coming peril, "Heavens, no! He's a disappearing pleasure!" When G.K.C. died, G.B.S. noted rather sadly that contact between them had been infrequent in recent years. Yet, G.B.S. took care to add quickly: "But of course we were very conscious of one another. I enjoyed him and admired him keenly and nothing could have been more generous than his treatment of me. Our controversies were exhibition spars in which nothing could have induced either of us to hurt the other."[1]

As late as his ninetieth year G.B.S. was to recall G.K.C. as one of his favorite verbal sparring partners. G.K.C. had been dead for a decade, but he remained one of the men with whom G.B.S. would most like to hold converse in an after-world. Shaw told Stephen Winsten: "The last person I want to talk to is [T. E.] Lawrence. Oscar Wilde, yes; Chesterton, yes, but not Lawrence."[2]

Clearly, the friendship had remained intact. What then had silenced the "Debaters of the Century"? Why had the debates ended suddenly? The answer is that the debates did not end abruptly. Actually, the controversy had come to a close rather gradually. By 1928, G.B.S. and G.K.C. were aware—as the public was not yet aware—that the basic controversy had long since reached its point of no return. In the early years G.B.S. and G.K.C. had insisted that the differences between them were genuine and irreconcilable. Abiding friendship and a willingness to "agree to differ" on a mature and understanding level had alone made the debates tenable. The Edwardian public had misled only itself when it tried to manufacture a false kinship of ideas between G.B.S. and G.K.C. Such an attempt had been natural. Both G.B.S. and G.K.C. did fling a sharp challenge at the public's existing values. Yet not once in the debates had G.B.S. or G.K.C. proposed a similar solution to any major problem that confronted English society. On the contrary, the debates, viewed as a unit, revealed that the solutions of G.B.S.– G.K.C. presented a neat study in contrasts.

The early G.K.C. had called vaguely for a Catholic Socialist State. Peasant proprietorship over private property was the nostrum to install peace and plenty in the land. The peace would be comfortably analogous to that G.K.C. was fond of ascribing to the Middle Ages. Predictably, G.B.S. had hooted at the Chestertonian ideal of rule by peasantry. Rather, the proletariat should take over the ownership of the means of production and exchange. Only collective ownership of major industries by the state could permit government to operate efficiently. At the time one could find much to debate in such diverse views. One could find no semblance of identity.

Nor did basic disagreement between G.B.S. and G.K.C. ever cause the controversy to grow static or meaningless. Activist Shaw was always forcing G.K.C. to rethink his position as the years rolled along. Under Shavian prodding

G.K.C. did move steadily away from the vague concept of a Catholic Socialist State to the tighter concept of a Catholic Distributism. G.K.C. had arrived on more tenable ground when he was able to contend that redistribution of segments of land to individual owners might better satisfy the instincts of men to own private property. Yet here, as always, when one had succeeded in effecting a change in the thinking of the other, the change only served to move the ultimate position of the two men further apart.

The one exception was science, a topic on which G.B.S. and G.K.C. seemed totally agreed. One might scoff at science because it *tried* to be a new religion. The other might scoff at science because it had *failed* to become a new religion. Whatever the motives, both derided the claims of science for their whole lifetimes. On all other questions the men were obviously poles apart. In 1928, Shaw was openly admiring eugenics as the rationalistic separation of sex and marriage. G.K.C. was to do more than to disparage the Shavian view. He was to pit against it nothing less than the Christian view of traditional family solidarity. This sort of reasoning had led the men more quickly to the point of no return. In politics, Shaw had honed his ideal of representative Fabian democracy into a subtle instrument. The Shavian voter had to meet the requirements of a complex set of educational and economic qualifications. By 1928, G.K.C. had decided to place his faith in a much more direct form of democracy. Chesterton's democracy demanded of its voters no educational or economic requirements whatever! Again, the dichotomy of viewpoint was complete.

It had always been in religious attitudes and beliefs that the contrast had been sharpest of all. As early as 1911, in "The Future of Religion" address, Shaw had cited the contemporary environment as the prime factor that had shaped his soul for the religion of the future. The intelligent contemporary man must eschew Biblical legends and build a religion that was individual and original. Even then, in 1911, G.K.C. had countered by maintaining that his own soul had been strengthened by an old religion in which the very miracles and divine grace inadmissible to G.B.S. had played a vital part. In 1922, the gap widened. G.K.C. was received into the Roman Catholic Church as a convert. Shaw admitted immediately that a Roman Catholic Chesterton was "incomprehensible" to him. The breaking point was near, but, remarkable fact, the friendly controversy endured another six years into 1928.

Perhaps something deeper than friendship had to exist to prolong the conflict over so long a span. That something might have been the profound satisfaction it afforded two intellectuals to discover that they were much more successful in communicating their ideas to the public when acting as catalysts upon one another. When sharing the same platform, G.B.S. and G.K.C. always did seem able to invent particularly apt epigrams and analogies to express their opposite views on the issues of the day. But now the fun was over. By 1928, years of subtle reasoning over the same issues had constricted fatally the areas open to dispute. No room was left for fresh and inventive argument. For artists like G.B.S. and G.K.C. that meant the debates had to end. The hour for artistic separation had come. G.B.S. and G.K.C. would not sustain the debates merely because the public was still laughing and appreciative and unaware that an aura of finality had settled on the shape of argument in the controversy. Once the end had come artistically, it had to come actually, as it did in 1928. For two such men, committed to opposite views of truth, how could it have been otherwise?

The controversy then had to end in permanent disagreement and it did end in permanent disagreement. But what of the personal friendship? Why had it slacked off?

Why were G.B.S. and G.K.C. only "occasionally in touch," as Vincent Brome puts it, between 1928 and 1936? This is a much more subtle area. Both men were rueful over the separation. When Katharine T. Clemens visited G.K.C., he pointed sadly at his Top Meadows fireplace and at two chairs "on which said Mr. Chesterton sometimes sat himself and his friend, Bernard Shaw. He told us that there were few of his contemporaries whom he liked better than George Bernard Shaw, but that they had met more in public than in private and generally on platforms which were put up for them to fight each other like two knockabout comedians."[3]

G.K.C. always seemed helpless to explain why he had not managed to spend more time in the company of such a "splendid" man as Shaw. Chesterton believed that when Shaw talked, food and drink were minor accessories. No one in his right senses would miss the opportunity to hear Bernard Shaw. It never seemed to occur to G.K.C. in his transparent innocence that some of his friends were not as avid as he for Shavian companionship. Nor, despite all his witticisms on the subject, did it ever seem to register with G.K.C. that Shaw's vegetarianism and abstemiousness were social realities. Shaw was hardly the man with whom G.K.C. and his rollicking Fleet Street coterie could share steaks and ale. Actually, this simple matter of dietetical tastes precluded Shaw's attendance at dozens of the very social functions which G.K.C. found most enjoyable.

Shaw, always the more practical of the two, had no such illusions. He, too, regretted that he did not see more of G.K.C. Yet he knew precisely why and how differences in temperament and taste kept them apart. He understood how society took a hand to insure that his relationship with G.K.C. should always remain more cerebral and literary than personal. Shaw explained the whole situation in a few sentences: "Our actual physical contacts, however, were few, as he never belonged to the Fabian society nor came to its meetings (this being my set), whilst his Fleet Street Bohemianism lay outside my vegetarian, teetotal, non-smoking tastes. Besides, he apparently liked literary society; and it had the grace to like him. I avoided it and it loathed me."[4]

Nevertheless, while the debates thrived, the two chairs before the fireplace at Top Meadow were at least sometimes filled. G.B.S. was not the man for small talk but he did enjoy meeting with G.K.C. to plan a new, or to rehash an old, public encounter. The meetings really were quite warm and human. G.K.C. would avoid the meringues filled with Devonshire cream that Frances was wont to serve and eat scones instead, making preposterous allusion to watching his weight as scone after scone disappeared. G.B.S. did induce G.K.C. to make one monumental sacrifice. In deference to Shaw, he drank only tea. Two cups were his limit. Still, G.B.S. might have argued facetiously that few men had affected the Chestertonian diet more.

For all the affection between them, there was little reason for the men to meet socially once the debates had ceased. G.B.S. always did need a cause and a reason to meet with anyone. His was indeed the genius for work and action, G.K.C.'s for friendship and enjoyment. At the same time, the friendship, as well as the controversy, had been prolonged by the stimuli of the work and the action. Between 1901 and 1913, G.B.S. had been fascinated with G.K.C.'s potential as dramatist. Many a social meeting had resulted from the fascination. G.B.S. liked to combine work and play. Between 1911 and 1928, the debates, formal and informal, written and oral, had helped to hold them together long after it had become evident that philosophically the twain could never meet. Art more than life became increasingly the link that sustained the friendship. William Irvine was to write almost too sweepingly: "They could not make themselves understood across the spiritual distance which separated them so that, like the public at large, they came more and more to admire each other as writers and to discount each other as thinkers."[5]

It is true that even by 1922, G.B.S. and G.K.C. had become quite vocal about discounting each other as thinkers. It is true that ostensibly they had come to meet only for reasons of art. Yet one wonders. Is it safe to make such distinctions concerning the intellectual history of the pair? Could two such brilliant men meet, argue art or anything else for hours on end and *not* affect each other's thinking? One must concede the paradoxical fact that, even after 1928, their ideas came together occasionally in a rush of solid agreement that shut off debate and controversy.

For example, G.B.S. had horrified all Socialists but not G.K.C. when he seemed to express approval of Monarchy in *The Apple Cart* (1929). Again, G.K.C. was not aghast when G.B.S. commenced to praise the Fascists in the early thirties. Instead, he sensed a wild consistency in Shaw's plea for order at any price. G.K.C. wrote confidently in 1935:

> *The Apple Cart* is important as showing how many million miles he [Shaw] is still ahead of the Progressives; how much more modern he is than the Modernists. He has realized that the really modern thing is Monarchy. It does not in the least follow that because it is the modern thing, it is the right thing . . . but at least Bernard Shaw in his old age is up-to-date. He understands the political change and challenge of our time. . . . Indeed his last political phase seems to be largely a general loathing of anarchy; and a disposition to accept whatever can reduce it to rational order, whether it be Fascism or Bolshevism.[6]

It was as though G.K.C. were welcoming G.B.S. home into a quieter and more conservative world when he praised *The Apple Cart*. G.B.S. would not have been surprised. His intuitive rapport with G.K.C. was quite keen. G.B.S. had understood all along G.K.C.'s kinship with the ideas in *The Apple Cart*. In March, 1930, he had written to Mrs. Chesterton: "There is a new play badly wanted for the Malvern Festival this year and I do not see how I can possibly find time to write it. A chance for Gilbert, who ought to have written *The Apple Cart*. He leaves everything to me nowadays."[7]

The fact that the two no longer met regularly by 1930 had not dulled G.B.S.'s powers of perception about G.K.C. For he was probably correct in assuming that G.K.C. could have written *The Apple Cart*. Chesterton was completely in accord with every essential idea in the play. G.K.C. would also have defended King Magnus against the loud, jingoistic Democrat just as Shaw had done. But in their mutual recognition of what was actually the central political problem of the play and the times in which the play was written, G.B.S. and G.K.C. would have demonstrated best their intellectual rapport. For Chesterton, too, would have realized that the conflict between Magnus and his Cabinet was minor compared to the conflict in which Magnus and his Cabinet must engage as allies against the real enemy, Plutocracy, which wanted to rule them both. Therefore, G.K.C.'s instinct would have been to fight, as did Shaw, Breakages Limited, which was the real antagonist of the play because it clearly represented the monopolistic and dictatorial rule of Capitalism. Never, not even in the early days of 1911, had G.B.S. come as close to G.K.C. ideologically, as when he wrote *The Apple Cart* in 1929.

After 1928 only the physical contact was to wane between G.B.S. and G.K.C. The intellectual rapport, although infrequently exercised, was to remain constant until the end. As a result, the basic structure of the friendship did not really change. For the intellectual rapport had always been the key to practical action in the case of G.B.S. and G.K.C. Actually it is startling to learn how often, by intellectual means alone, these men were able to affect one another in the practical areas of life. Other friends might need personal contact to effect such changes; G.B.S. and G.K.C. did not. The two depended upon pure mind to an extent that would have pleased a Plato.

At the same time the intellectual rapport was not of that variety that can be described as cold and unfeeling. Rather, it continued warm and vital to the end. When G.K.C. died in 1936, G.B.S. was to remember immediately that his friend had been most unworldly about money and a writer who was generally underpaid. On the very next day he wrote to Mrs. Chesterton: "It seems the most ridiculous thing in the world that I, eighteen years older than Gilbert should be heartlessly surviving him. However, this is only to say that if you have any temporal bothers that I can remove, a line on a post card (or three figures) will be sufficient. The trumpets are sounding for him; and the slightest interruption must be intolerable. Faithfully, G.B.S."[8] Frances was financially solvent but she was immensely moved by G.B.S.'s instant solicitude for her when he heard of her husband's death. Intellectual challenge had always been only one side of what G.B.S. and G.K.C. had provided for one another. The other side was genuine friendship.

Life had meant much more to this pair than perpetual argument and debate. Occasionally, the two had managed to come together in a meeting of minds as when Shaw published his "Chestertonian" play *The Apple Cart* (1929). Yet neither had ever really expected agreement from the other. The dialogue had been ecumenical half a century before the word became fashionable.

The hour of their fame as friends and rivals waits only that hour when G.K.C. becomes fashionable again as G.B.S. has remained fashionable, i.e., written about, read, and revived on the stage. Even Shaw suffered a brief dip in reputation after his death. The human race does seem to have this perverse tendency to despise its grandfather but to worship Plato. Predictably, G.B.S. did not remain out of sight for long. The Shavian artistry proved too protean and soon a whole new generation was chuckling over G.B.S. Different generations may well return to different facets of Shaw. Yet Shaw, himself, as the cliché goes, seems certain to survive as long as the English speaking stage survives. The critical comment that rates G.B.S. "the best British dramatist since Shakespeare" has already become fixed as a truism.

The literary fate of G.K.C. presents a more complex and puzzling problem. G.K.C. was as multi-faceted an artist as G.B.S. Although he did not do his basic work, as had G.B.S., in quite so popular a medium as the drama, much that G.K.C. wrote in media as public as the novel and the daily newspaper was both popular and memorable. Actually, G.K.C. has been—even more than Shaw—the most quoted British writer of the twentieth century. As Garry Wills wrote of G.K.C.: "On scales we cannot wield, he may be, even now, one of the world's most influential writers."[9] Yet G.K.C.'s books do not sell all that well, and, until recently, he has languished most where one might have expected it least—among professional students and scholars. Still, even this latter fact is understandable. G.K.C. did pose a special problem for students and scholars just as he always had for librarians and booksellers. James S. Kortendick, S.S., summed up that problem when he wrote:

> He [G.K.C.] was a much greater literary figure than his current literary reputation would suggest. . . . If we find fewer references to him in the quarterlies and the new books, the reasons are likely to be found in the great diversity of his work and the unmanageability of his almost unbelievable range. . . . In a library or bookshop

he must be hunted through shelves marked History, Biography, Travel, Criticism, Essays, etc. It is impossible to put him in any one literary slot. . . . In an age of specialists, or authorities in particular subjects, or in type of literary form, we find ourselves less comfortable with the "universal man."[10]

G.K.C. began to achieve a scholarly revival in 1958 (twenty-two years after his death) when John Sullivan published the first full-scale bibliography of his works. Although Sullivan filled a basic need, the gap in Chesterton studies closed even more impressively in 1966 when Joseph W. Sprug published *An Index to G. K. Chesterton*. After laboring since the early fifties, Sprug had succeeded in indexing the heterogeneous writings of G.K.C. in the social, political, religious, and literary fields. At last it was possible to get at the essence of G.K.C. with relative ease. G.K.C. has fared better of late. In fact, where editorial acumen, selectivity, and range are concerned, the latest of his posthumous anthologies, *Spice of Life* (1965), happens to be the best published in many years.

Recently, G.K.C. has also been attracting a more dramatic and unexpected kind of public notice than accrues to anthologies and reprints. The latest instance occurred early in the summer of 1968. London's Mermaid Theatre was housing one of its biggest hits in years when the management announced: "In addition to the nightly performance of the smash hit play 'Hadrian VII,' the Mermaid is mounting three programmes for the 1968 City Festival." The first of the programs was to deal with one of the "great English poets." The great English "poet" turned out to be G. K. Chesterton! John Turner and Gerald Frow, who staged the lively program, were wise enough to include readings from G.K.C.'s essays as well as from his poetry. Again, the actors complemented the readings with an enactment of scenes from the life of "this intensely English author." The Chesterton segment of the City Festival of London played The Mermaid on the evenings of July 15, 19, and 24, 1968. Ironically, Shaw got into the act once more. The Mermaid playbill advertising Chesterton quoted G.B.S. without crediting him, when it announced: "A programme in the life and works of a gusty Englishman 'who might be trusted anywhere without a policeman.'" Shaw made that observation in the "Chesterbelloc" essay of 1905.

Events such as that at the Mermaid exhilarate Chestertonians. Still, it seems idle to speculate too long on the mere direction from which the Chesterton revival will spring. The truth is that any one of the G.K.C.'s—the probing literary critic, the artist of the fantastic novels, the poet in soaring Gothic come most quickly to mind—could be the first one to come back into popular favor. The Chesterton revival will certainly come. As Garry Wills wrote in 1962: "Men predict a rebirth, or the emergence from obscuring historical accidents of a 'real' Chesterton. That kind of rebirth will no doubt come. Chesterton is so far 'out' he is constantly in danger of becoming 'in.'"[11]

The preliminaries to G.K.C.'s revival have been accomplished. Scholars like Sullivan and Sprug have helped. So has Wills. All the omens are good. A poet as prominent as W. H. Auden announced recently that he is at work compiling an anthology of "G. K. Chesterton's idea stuff." Novelist Kingsley Amis devoted a whole page in the New York Times Book Review for October 13, 1968, to a favorable criticism and reminiscence of a single Chestertonian novel, The Man Who Was Thursday. So it goes. Apparently the topical encumbrances of G.K.C., the journalist, and G.K.C., the polemicist, have faded sufficiently to reveal the artist whom G.B.S.

called "a man of colossal genius." Surely the rest of the machinery of revival must be left up to the publishers, the public, and the vagaries of Lady Immortality.

An "in" Chesterton could stir up the pot. Shaw-Chesterton alone might then occupy critics of the period for years to come. Teams of such stature are rare in literature and tend to raise many ponderables. To cite a single instance, one might speculate long on how much to credit art and how much to credit the magnanimity of the artists for a friendship-rivalry that endured thirty-five years. Where talents were so strikingly similar but beliefs so diametrically different, that apparently simple question becomes difficult to answer. As G.K.C. once wrote: "The best sort of critic draws attention not to the finality of a thing but to its infinity. Instead of closing a question, he opens a hundred." This pair were themselves of a magnitude to invite such speculation. The largeness with which Shaw and Chesterton treated one another could well serve as a hallmark for their treatment by others.

notes · bibliography · index

notes

PREFACE

1. Maisie Ward, *Gilbert Keith Chesterton* (New York, 1943), p. 220.
2. Maisie Ward, *Return to Chesterton* (New York, 1952), p. xi.

one
·
"WHAT ABOUT THE PLAY?"

1. Vincent Brome, *Six Studies In Quarreling* (London, 1958), p. 138.
2. Ward, *G.K.C.,* p. 154.
3. Shaw himself mentioned the 1906 meeting with Rodin in a book review (*The Nation,* Nov. 9, 1912, p. 259) and in his letters. See also the notebooks of Rodin and two letters of Rainer Maria Rilke dated April 19, 1906, in which Rilke gave an account of a day spent watching Rodin modeling Shaw.
4. George Bernard Shaw, "A Generous Opponent," *The Mark Twain Quarterly,* I (spring, 1937), 9.
5. Ward, *G.K.C.,* p. 155.
6. Archibald Henderson, *George Bernard Shaw: Man of the Century* (New York, 1956), p. 791.
7. See the photograph of Rodin's sculpture in Henderson's book. Epstein did a better work on Shaw (also pictured in Henderson) in later years, but Rodin caught him at the right age.
8. Stanley Weintraub, *Private Shaw and Public Shaw* (London, 1963), pp. 1–30.
9. Hilaire Belloc, *On the Place of G. K. Chesterton in English Letters* (New York, 1940).
10. George Bernard Shaw, "The Chesterbelloc," *Pen Portraits and Reviews* (London, 1949), pp. 71–81.

11. Ward, *G.K.C.*, p. 226.

12. Their sprightly character makes Shaw's letters a valuable literary by-product of the association of the two men. Chesterton's, however, were sporadic, usually undated, slapdash, and obviously written in great haste.

13. Ward, *G.K.C.*, pp. 234–36.

14. *Ibid.*, pp. 239–40.

15. *Ibid.*, p. 369.

16. Frank Harris, *Contemporary Portraits* (New York, 1920), pp. 65–66.

17. Mrs. Cecil Chesterton, *The Chestertons* (London, 1941), p. 132.

18. Ward, *G.K.C.*, pp. 369–70.

19. Mrs. Cecil Chesterton, pp. 134–35.

20. George Bernard Shaw, "The Case Against Chesterton," *The New Statesman*, VII (May 13, 1916), 136.

21. Ward, *G.K.C.*, pp. 240–41.

22. G. K. Chesterton, *G.K.C as M.C.: Thirty-Seven Introductions*, ed. J. P. de Fonseka (London, 1929), pp. 66–67.

23. Garry Wills, *Chesterton: Man and Mask* (New York, 1961), p. 205.

24. G. K. Chesterton, *The Surprise*, with a preface by Dorothy L. Sayers (New York, 1953), p. 9.

25. Ward, *G.K.C.*, p. 229.

26. Wills, *Man and Mask*, pp. 125–27. Mr. Wills has noted this as well as many of the stylistic and theatrical resemblances between G.B.S. and G.K.C. which are worked out in some detail in the pages which follow.

27. George Bernard Shaw, *Shaw on Theatre*, ed. E. J. West (New York, 1961), p. 166.

28. Wills, *Man and Mask*, p. 119.

29. See *The Trial of John Jasper for the Murder of Edwin Drood: Report of the Proceedings from the Shorthand Notes of W. T. Ley* (London, 1914).

30. George Bernard Shaw, letter to George Cornwallis West, British Museum, folio no. 50517.

31. G. K. Chesterton, *Autobiography* (New York, 1936), pp. 237–40.

32. *Ibid.*, pp. 236–37.

33. Evelyn Waugh, *Monsignor Ronald Knox* (Boston, 1959), pp. 207–8.

34. Benedictines of Stanbrook Abbey, *In a Great Tradition* (New York, 1956), p. 274.

35. *Ibid.*, p. 277.

two
•
G.K.C.'S *GEORGE BERNARD SHAW*

1. St. John Ervine, *Bernard Shaw: His Life, Work and Friends* (London, 1956), p. viii.
2. Ward, *G.K.C.,* p. 237. This criticism originally appeared in *The Bystander,* September 1907.
3. G. K. Chesterton, *George Bernard Shaw* (London, 1948), pp. 228–29.
4. Bernard Shaw, "Review of *George Bernard Shaw* by G. K. Chesterton," *Pen Portraits and Reviews* (London, 1949), pp. 81–89. Shaw's review first appeared in *The Nation* on August 23, 1909. The review was admired, and Shaw himself selected it for hard cover permanence in the 1949 collection.
5. In the collection of the Houghton Library, Harvard University.
6. British Museum folio 50562.
7. Hesketh Pearson, *G.B.S.: A Full Length Portrait* (New York, 1942), p. 280.
8. Pearson, *Full Length Portrait,* pp. 315–16.
9. G. K. Chesterton, *St. Thomas Aquinas* (Garden City, New York, 1957), p. 11.
10. Christopher Hollis, *G. K. Chesterton* (London, 1950), p. 20.
11. G.K.C., *Shaw,* p. 1.
12. *Ibid.,* pp. 79–80.
13. *Ibid.,* p. 99.
14. H. M. Geduld, "Place and Treatment of Persons in *Back to Methuselah,*" *The California Shavian,* v (November-December, 1964), 1.
15. G. K. Chesterton, *George Bernard Shaw* (London, 1909), p. 1. This passage appears only in the introduction to the first edition.
16. *Ibid.,* pp. 11–12.

three
•
GENESIS OF "THE DEBATERS OF THE CENTURY"

1. Shaw, *Platform and Pulpit,* ed. Dan H. Laurence (New York, 1961), p. xiv.
2. Shaw, *Sixteen Self Sketches* (New York, 1949), p. 101.
3. Cyril Clemens, *Chesterton, as Seen by His Contemporaries* (Webster Groves, Missouri, 1939), p. 66.

4. *Ibid.*, pp. 66–67.
5. *Ibid.*, p. 68.
6. Wills, *Man and Mask*, pp. 116–17.
7. St. John G. Ervine, *Some Impressions of My Elders* (New York, 1922), pp. 92–93.
8. Frank Swinnerton, "A Beautiful Character," *The Mark Twain Quarterly*, I (spring, 1937), 9.

four

·

THE FIRST PUBLIC ENCOUNTERS

1. Brome, p. 147.
2. Bernard Shaw, "The Future of Religion," sometimes titled "The Religion of the Future," as in Warren Smith's *The Religious Speeches of Bernard Shaw* (University Park, Pa., 1963).
3. Chesterton, *George Bernard Shaw* (1948 ed.), pp. 84–85.
4. Shaw, *Sixteen Self-Sketches*, pp. 159–60.
5. G.K.C., *Shaw*, p. 71.
6. J. Percy Smith, *The Unrepentant Pilgrim: A Study of the Development of Bernard Shaw* (Boston, 1965), p. 252.
7. All quotations of this speech are from Bernard Shaw, *Religious Speeches of Bernard Shaw,* ed. Warren S. Smith (University Park, Pa., 1963), pp. 29–36.
8. The precise moments at which Shaw employed his characteristic movements and gestures in this particular speech are now impossible to verify, but all other descriptive material such as crowd size, Shaw's exact words, etc. are completely verifiable and have been checked.
9. Both quotations from *G. K. Chesterton's Reply to Bernard Shaw* —a pamphlet privately printed for the Cambridge Heretics and graciously forwarded to this writer by Miss Dorothy Collins, G.K.C.'s literary executrix.
10. *G.K.C.'s Reply*, pp. 4–7.
11. G.K.C.'s precise weight was the one subject about which he was always to be reticent, e.g., "Madame, my height is 6'2". No scale has ever been able to calculate my weight." Mr. John Mangan, his chauffeur at Notre Dame, Indiana, 1931–32, said flatly, "He was close to 400 lbs., but he'd never give it away."
12. *Return to Chesterton*, p. 271.
13. *Religious Speeches*, p. xviii.

14. All quotations are from *G.K.C.'s Reply.*
15. *The Cambridge Daily News* for November 18, 1911; quoted in *G.K.C.'s Reply.*
16. *The Gownsman* for November 25, 1911; quoted in *G.K.C.'s reply.*
17. Brome, p. 154.

five
•
DEBATES—FORMAL AND INFORMAL

1. Ward, *G.K.C.,* p. 365.
2. Henderson, p. 845.
3. Brome, pp. 147–48.
4. All quotations of this debate are from Shaw, *Platform and Pulpit,* pp. 86–93. Ironically, the first debate has only become available to the general public in recent years. The first debate was published last and the last debate was published first. Not until 1961 did Dan H. Laurence resurrect the first debate for his *Platform and Pulpit.* Working from Dec. 6 and Dec. 13, 1911, issues of the "Christian Commonwealth," Laurence was able to publish the bulk of what G.B.S. and G.K.C. actually said in "The Democrat, The Socialist, and The Gentleman."
5. Anne Fremantle, *This Little Band of Prophets: The British Fabians* (New York, 1960), p. 169.
6. Ward, *G.K.C.,* p. 565.
7. Louis Biancolli, *The Book of Great Conversations* (New York, 1948), p. 499.
8. This and all the quotations of the conversation are from *Great Conversations,* pp. 498–506.
9. William Irvine, *The Universe of G.B.S.* (New York, London, Toronto, 1949), p. 340.
10. Bernard Shaw, "The Case Against Chesterton," p. 133.
11. Father Dempsey and Father Keegan: two Irish priests whom Shaw had created in *John Bull's Other Island* (1904) to reflect his views on the Roman Catholic Church.
12. Ward, *G.K.C.,* pp. 489–90.
13. Irvine, *The Universe of G.B.S.,* p. 341.
14. W. R. Titterton, *G. K. Chesterton: A Portrait* (London, 1947), p. 102.
15. *Ibid.,* p. 183.
16. Marie H. Nichols, *Rhetoric and Criticism* (Baton Rouge, La., 1963), p. 128.

17. Brome, p. 161.
18. Titterton, p. 183.
19. Maisie Ward, *Return to Chesterton*, p. 263.
20. Titterton, *Chesterton*, p. 184.
21. Ward, *Return*, p. 272.
22. Hesketh Pearson, *Lives of the Wits* (New York and Evanston, 1962), p. xii.
23. *Ibid.*, p. 286. Hilaire Belloc and Max Beerbohm were such a disparate pair that few would have picked them to become good friends. Yet Beerbohm was one of the few men Belloc liked without reservation.
24. All quotations from G. K. Chesterton and Bernard Shaw, *A Debate with Hilaire Belloc in the Chair: Do We Agree?* (New York, 1964).
25. Pearson, *Lives,* p. 270.
26. Irvine, *The Universe of G.B.S.*, p. 340.
27. *Ibid.*
28. Eric Bentley, *Bernard Shaw* (London, 1950), p. 49.
29. G.B.S. is obviously referring to G.K.C.'s Father Brown mysteries. He pinpoints Chesterton's literary techniques unerringly.
30. Chesterton's obvious reference to Shaw's *Back to Methuselah* (1921) has never been quoted in a resumé of the debate before, probably because it is not particularly important within the context of the subject matter of this debate. However, the reference is of genuine significance to anyone tracing the Shaw-Chesterton literary relationship. *Back to Methuselah* was such a key work in G.K.C.'s estimation that after 1921 he seems never to have engaged in a prolonged piece of writing or speaking about Shaw without making a reference to it.
31. Titterton, p. 187.
32. Brome, p. 168.

six
•
A NEW GLIMPSE OF *METHUSELAH*

1. Shaw, *Self-Sketches*, pp. 119–29.
2. *Ibid.*, p. 125.
3. Bernard Shaw, Introduction to *Back to Methuselah* (London, 1931), xx–xxi.
4. *Ibid.*

5. *Ibid.*

6. *Ibid.*

7. G.K.C., *Shaw,* p. 285. (Quoted from "The Later Phases," the chapter G.K.C. appended to *George Bernard Shaw* in 1935.)

8. "A Glimpse of the Domesticity of Franklin Barnabas," appeared in the volume *Short Stories, Scraps and Shavings* (New York, 1932).

9. H. M. Geduld, "Place and Treatment of Persons in *Back to Methuselah" The California Shavian,* V (November–December 1964), 11.

10. *Scraps and Shavings,* p. 141. Unless otherwise noted, all quotations for the rest of this chapter are from *Scraps and Shavings.*

11. Irvine, *Universe,* p. 342.

12. The rejection of the apostrophe in "don't," and other Shavian idiosyncrasies in punctuation and spelling give evidence in *Scraps and Shavings* that G.B.S. had close control over the Ayot St. Lawrence edition of his *Collected Works.*

13. Similarly, G.K.C. had no ear for music. G.B.S., who played the piano for him, used to chide him for his lack of appreciation.

14. In the Fleet Street days, many a journalist was pleased to see one of his conversations with G.K.C. leap into print as an article. In the portrait of Immenso, G.B.S. had included almost every facet of G.K.C.'s *modus operandi.*

15. Arthur Gelb, "Our Men in the Balcony," *The Shaw Society of Chicago Newsletter,* III (May, 1960), 3, quoted from *The New York Times,* March 8, 1960.

seven
•

THE LAST PHASE, 1928–36

1. Bernard Shaw, "A Generous Opponent," *The Mark Twain Quarterly,* I (spring, 1937), 9.

2. Weintraub, p. 280.

3. Katharine T. Clemens, "Chesterton at Top Meadow," *The Mark Twain Quarterly,* I (spring, 1937), 13.

4. Shaw, "A Generous Opponent," p. 9. Apparently G.B.S., writing in 1937, forgot momentarily that before 1900, during the Boer war, G.K.C. had served a brief turn as a Fabian Socialist. However, since Chesterton had never found the Fabians congenial, the substance of G.B.S.'s comment is correct.

5. Irvine, pp. 337–38.

6. G. K. Chesterton, *George Bernard Shaw* (London, 1948), p. 262, in "The Later Phases," a chapter written specially in 1935 for this edition of the book.

7. Bernard Shaw to Mrs. Frances Chesterton, unpublished letter, 10 March 1930, in possession of Dorothy Collins, Chesterton's literary executrix. Quoted with the permission of the Society of Authors.

8. Quoted in Brome, p. 190.

9. Garry Wills, "The Secret Festival" (A Chesterton Anniversary), *The Catholic Book Reporter* (April–May, 1962), p. 6.

10. Joseph W. Sprug, ed., *An Index to G. K. Chesterton* (Washington, D.C., 1966), p. vii.

11. Wills, "Secret Festival," p. 6.

bibliography

Amis, Kingsley. "Speaking of Books: 'The Man Who Was Thursday,' " *The New York Times Book Review,* October 13, 1968.

Belloc, Hilaire. *On the Place of G. K. Chesterton in English Letters.* New York, 1940.

Benedictines of Stanbrook Abbey. *In A Great Tradition.* New York, 1956.

Bentley, Eric. *Bernard Shaw.* London, 1950.

Biancolli, Louis, ed. *The Book of Great Conversations.* New York, 1948.

Brome, Vincent. *Six Studies in Quarreling.* London, 1958.

Chesterton, Mrs. Cecil. *The Chestertons.* London, 1941.

Chesterton, G. K. *The Autobiography of G. K. Chesterton.* New York, 1936.

_____. *Eugenics and Other Evils.* London, 1922.

_____. *Father Brown Mystery Stories,* ed. Raymond T. Bond. New York, 1962.

_____. *The Future of Religion: Mr. G. K. Chesterton's Reply to Mr. Bernard Shaw* [apparently Cambridge, 1911 or 1912].

_____. *George Bernard Shaw.* London, 1909 (2nd ed. 1948).

_____. *G.K.C. as M.C.: Thirty-Seven Introductions,* ed. J. P. de Fonseka. London, 1929.

_____. *G.K.'s Weekly.* London, 1934.

_____. *Heretics.* London and New York, 1905.

_____. *The Judgment of Dr. Johnson.* New York and London, 1928.

_____. *Magic: A Fantastic Comedy.* London, 1913.

_____. *The Man Who Was Thursday.* New York, 1960.

_____. *The Napoleon of Notting Hill.* London, 1904.

_____. *Orthodoxy.* London, 1909.

_____. *St. Francis of Assisi.* New York, 1958.

_____. *St. Thomas Aquinas.* Garden City, N.Y., 1957.

_____. *Spice of Life.* Beaconsfield, Bucks, England, 1965.

_____. *The Surprise,* with a preface by Dorothy L. Sayers. New York, 1953.

_____. *The Trial of John Jasper for the Murder of Edwin Drood:*

Report of the Proceedings from the Shorthand Notes of W. T. Ley. London, 1914.

Chesterton, G. K., and Bernard Shaw. *A Debate with Hilaire Belloc in the Chair: Do We Agree?* New York, 1964.

Clemens, Cyril C. *Chesterton as Seen by His Contemporaries.* Webster Groves, Missouri (International Mark Twain Society), 1939.

Clemens, Katharine T. "Chesterton at Top Meadow," *The Mark Twain Quarterly,* I (spring 1937), 13.

Duffin, H. C. *The Quintessence of Bernard Shaw.* London, 1939.

Ervine, St. John. *Bernard Shaw: His Life, Work and Friends.* London, 1956.

_____. "Portrait of Bernard Shaw," *The Listener,* LIV (August 18, 1955), 249.

_____. *Some Impressions of My Elders.* New York, 1922.

Fremantle, Anne. *This Little Band of Prophets: The British Fabians.* New York, 1960.

Geduld, H. M. "Place and Treatment of Persons in *Back to Methuselah,*" *The California Shavian,* V (November–December 1964), 1–12.

Harris, Frank. *Contemporary Portraits: (Third Series).* New York, 1920.

Henderson, Archibald. *George Bernard Shaw: Man of the Century.* New York, 1956.

Hollis, Christopher. *G. K. Chesterton.* London (Supplement to *British Book News*), 1950.

Irvine, William. *The Universe of G.B.S.* New York, London, Toronto, 1949.

McCarthy, Lillah. *Myself and My Friends.* New York, 1933.

Mark Twain Quarterly. Special Chesterton Number, spring 1937.

Nichols, Marie Hochmuth. *Rhetoric and Criticism.* Baton Rouge, Louisiana, 1963.

Pearson, Hesketh. *Bernard Shaw: His Life and Personality.* New York, 1963.

_____. *G.B.S.: A Full Length Portrait.* New York, 1942.

_____. *Lives of the Wits.* New York and Evanston, 1962.

Pegis, Anton G. "An Appreciation," a preface to *Saint Thomas Aquinas* by G. K. Chesterton. New York, 1957.

Rilke, Rainer Maria. *Selected Letters,* ed. Harry T. Moore. Garden City, N.Y., 1960.

Shaw, G. B. *Back to Methuselah.* London, 1931.

_____. *Bernard Shaw, Collected Letters: 1874–1897,* ed. Dan H. Laurence. New York, 1965.

_____. "The Case Against Chesterton," *The New Statesman,* VII (May 13, 1916), 133–36.

_____. *The Collected Works of Bernard Shaw,* Ayot St. Lawrence Edition, 30 vols. New York, 1932.

_____. *Complete Plays with Prefaces,* 6 vols. New York, 1962.

_____. "Dialogue of the Devil and St. Augustine," unpublished scenario, October, 1909. Holograph ms. and typescript carbon are in the Shaw Archives in the British Museum.

————. "A Generous Opponent," *The Mark Twain Quarterly*, I (spring, 1937), 9.

————. *Man and Superman*. Baltimore, 1962.

————. "A Memory of Rodin," *The Nation* (London), November 9, 1912, 259–60.

————. *Pen Portraits and Reviews*. London, 1949.

————. *Platform and Pulpit*, ed. Dan H. Laurence. New York, 1961.

————. *The Quintessence of G.B.S.*, ed. Stephen Winston. New York, 1949.

————. *The Religious Speeches of Bernard Shaw*, ed. Warren S. Smith. University Park, Pa., 1963.

————. *Shaw on Music*, ed. Eric Bentley. New York, 1955.

————. *Shaw on Theatre*, ed. E. J. West. New York, 1961.

————. *Short Stories, Scraps and Shavings*. New York, 1932.

————. *Sixteen Self Sketches*. New York, 1949.

————. Unpublished letter to Mrs. Frances Chesterton, 10 March 1930, in possession of Dorothy Collins, Chesterton's literary executrix.

Smith, J. Percy. *The Unrepentant Pilgrim: A Study of the Development of Bernard Shaw*. Boston, 1965.

Sprug, Joseph W., ed. *An Index to G. K. Chesterton*. Washington, D.C., 1966.

Stokes, E. E. "Bernard Shaw's Debt to John Bunyan," *Shaw Review*, VII (May 1965), 47

Sullivan, John. *G. K. Chesterton: A Bibliography*. London, 1958.

Swinnerton, Frank. *Background with Chorus*. London, 1956.

————. *Swinnerton, an Autobiography*. New York, 1936.

Titterton, W. R. *G. K. Chesterton: A Portrait*. London, 1947.

Ward, Maisie. *Gilbert Keith Chesterton*. New York, 1943.

————. *Return to Chesterton*. New York, 1952.

Waugh, Evelyn. *Monsignor Ronald Knox*. Boston, 1959.

Weintraub, Stanley. *Private Shaw and Public Shaw*. London, 1963.

West, Julius. *G. K. Chesterton: A Critical Study,* London, 1915.

Wills, Garry. *Chesterton: Man and Mask*. New York, 1961.

————. "The Secret Festival (A Chesterton Anniversary)," *Catholic Book Reporter*, II (April–May 1962), 5–6.

index